THIS BOOK

IS

Dedicated to the people of Ulster

In remembrance of those
who have given their lives
for their King and Country.

WITH
THE ULSTER DIVISION IN FRANCE.

A STORY OF THE 11th BATTALION ROYAL IRISH RIFLES (South Antrim Volunteers),

From BORDON to THIEPVAL.

IN FOUR PARTS,
INCLUDING PHOTOGRAPHS AND MAPS.

BY

A. P. I. S. AND D. G. S.

11
QUIS SEPARABIT

" The sequel of to-day unsolders all
The goodliest fellowship of famous knights
Whereof this world holds record:
Such a sleep they sleep—the men I loved,
I think that we shall never more, at any future time,
Delight our souls with talk of knightly deeds
Walking about the gardens and the halls
Of Camelot, as in the days that were."

From " The Passing of Arthur."
—LORD TENNYSON.

BELFAST:
WILLIAM MULLAN & SON, 4 DONEGALL PLACE.

THE KING REVIEWING THE ULSTER DIVISION

PREFACE.

The appearance of this little book needs a word of explanation. While at the front with the Ulster Division, the late Captain A. P. I. Samuels, had kept a very complete record of events, and collected all the material available, with the object of being in a position, some day, to publish an account of the doings of the Division, and particularly of his own Battalion, the 11th Royal Irish Rifles (South Antrim Volunteers.) It has been willed, however, that he should not be spared to carry out his intention. Like so many of his gallant comrades he gave his life for his country, being killed in action on September 24th, 1916. His name is now on Ulster's Roll of Honour, among those whose death has brought unspeakable grief to thousands of our homes, and yet has filled the hearts of Ulstermen and women with pride, and bequeathed such renown to our Province as will last while it endures. His papers, and the materials he had gathered have naturally come into my hands, and I have endeavoured, though in a very small and inadequate manner, to carry out the purpose for which they were collected.

This little book does not profess to be in any way a history of the Ulster Division, nor even of the 11th Batt. Royal Irish Rifles. Being compiled from the diary of Captain Samuels, supplemented by the records he was able to obtain, its scope is necessarily limited, and the story closes with the historic advance of the Ulster Division on the Somme at Thiepval on 1st July, 1916. In some respects this necessary limitation is a fitting one. To many in Ulster this great event marks in reality the passing of the glorious Division recruited during the first six months of the war, trained by Battalions in various camps in Ireland, and finally, as a Complete Division, at Seaford and Borden, before being sent to France. True, those permitted to survive that awful shock of July 1st, and those drafts in reserve at home remained to carry the fame of Ulster to Messines Ridge and Cambrai, but the Division was never again quite the same as before that memorable day. At that time it was unique. All its members were identified with the Northern Province. Each Battalion was recruited from some particular part, and even small districts and villages were represented separately in the Companies and Platoons. It was inevitable that after the Somme battle distinctive units should become merged, and that as the war progressed officers and men should find their way to the 36th Division who were not strictly representative of Ulster.

It is hoped that these memoirs may be of interest to Ulster people as describing the everyday life of a unit of their Division during its first eight months in France before the novelty of the life in billets and in trenches had worn off, and become merely monotonous, and while the point of view was still that of the native Ulsterman rather than the British soldier.

PART I.

We fell in at 4 o'clock on the afternoon of October 4, 1915, on the parade ground of St. Lucia Barracks, Borden. So mechanical a proceeding is a regimental parade, and so extremely heavy were the packs that we carried, that there was little opportunity for pondering over the changed conditions that we were soon to undergo. As far as the men were concerned—and the same applied to a large number of the officers—they had left their homes and all that home implied when they left Ireland three months before.

As we marched to the station we were struck by the apathy displayed by the few civilians we saw. There was no cheering, waving of handkerchiefs, or kissing of hands; even the children, making mud pies on the side of the road did not trouble to look up. We were only one of the many units that had passed down that same road during the previous fourteen months. It was almost an everyday sight now for the people who lived there to see regiments entraining for France. So it was, that as we marched down the short road to Borden station, we felt that we were only going on our business, and that those plain-clothed civilians—many of them young and physically fit men—were going on theirs. At Borden station the somewhat questionable spirits of the men were revived by large cups of excellent tea, brought round by ladies, a parting kindness which was greatly appreciated, and which none of us will f rget. The first train, with Brigade Headquarters, Battalion Head-quarters, and A and B Companies, steamed out of the station at 5-10 p.m., followed at 5-35 by the second train with C and D Companies. Blinds were drawn in the carriages soon after starting, and with only one stop the train ran through to Folkestone Pier, where we went on board the transport " Onward." At 9-35 p.m. we left the shores of England, bound for France and the unknown. A war-time cross-channel steamer, converted into a troopship for short runs, is as uncomfortable a

THE REVIEW OF THE ULSTER DIVISION.

form of craft as one can wish to sail in, and the
"Onward" was no exception to the rule. In addition
to our battalion there were several drafts, principally
from Scotch regiments, on board. Luckily it was a fine,
warm night, and the sea was as smooth as glass. The
dining-room and lounge were boarded up and stripped
as bare as a barrack floor, while the corridors, and every
available inch of accommodation below were packed
with men, in all those extraordinary attitudes, re-
cumbent and sprawling, which the sleeping Tommy can
only adopt. On deck it was just the same, and quite
impossible to walk from one end of the boat to the other.
There were strict orders against smoking on deck, and
the task of the unfortunate officer, whose sense of duty
was sufficiently strong to prevent him from winking at
any breach of discipline, was unenviable. A cigarette,
like Nerissa's candle, throws a long beam, and every
effort to reach the culprit was fraught with such curses
and mutterings from the bodies over which one stumbled,
that it would have disheartened even the adamant spirit
of the Secretary for War himself.

We reached Boulogne at 11-30 p.m., and, after the
usual disembarkation formalities, in which the
Disembarkation Officers and R.T.O.'s always seem to
exercise their unlimited powers to the full, the Battalion
fell in by companies about 300 yards down the pier. In
the darkness and heavy rain which now began to fall
this proceeding took a considerable amount of time, but
after half an hour we moved off, all thoroughly soaked
through. At the best of times the way from the pier
at Boulogne to the Rest Camp, some distance out of the
town, is not pleasant, but that October night it was
particularly bad. The streets were wet and slippery,
the men heavily laden with blankets and equipment,
and the road up to the Rest Camp led up a steep incline.
The leading company however, stepped out at their
normal pace. A few, mindful of the landing of the
original Expeditionary Force, and the ever famous
"Tipperary" scenes, burst into song, but the Frenchman retires early to bed, and, with the exception of one
long, thin arm fluttering a pocket handkerchief from a

top window, we saw no sign of life in the deserted streets. After a very steep climb of about two miles, we came to the Rest Camp, and a series of gasoline flares lit up the muddy flats on which the tents were pitched. The mud, ankle deep, sucked up round our boots, and torrents of rain danced in the puddles. It was a matter of ten minutes before each company was allotted its area, and after that, in less time than it takes to tell, the sleep, which only those who have spent a night in a Rest Camp at Boulogne know, had fallen on all.

The day after we landed was an easy one. No orders came as to moving, and the time was spent by our men in parading about the camp, sleeping, and talking to the numerous women and small boys who wandered round the railings, clamouring for " biscuit," " penny," or " bully beef." So urgent was the appeal for these commodities, that the men took it for granted that the entire population of France was starving, and handed over that somewhat elusive " unconsumed portion " of the previous day's ration, or any that remained of it. As the day wore on and word was received that there would be no move until the following morning, some of the officers were allowed into town in the afternoon. Boulogne in war-time is not an interesting place, and an hour was sufficient for exploration purposes. With the exception of a few French territorials, guarding the bridges and railway station, the town seemed to be entirely handed over to the British, whose motor ambulances glided in every direction. The " Cambria," with her green and white topsides and large Red Cross flag at her masthead, lay alongside at the quay, a sight to make one home-sick, which brought one's mind back to Dublin Bay and Kingstown Harbour in the days of peace. It rained off and on all day, and was bitterly cold, an early foretaste of the bitter winds we were to experience in France. We fell in next morning, Wednesday, 6th October, at 10-15, and marched to the Central station, where we entrained. Speculation was rife as to where we were going, whether Belgium, which savoured of Ypres and all that that name implied, or the new line between Arras and the Somme. The latter was a sector taken over by the British from the French in the July preceding, and had the name of being quiet and pleasant compared to the more northerly parts of the line. As the day wore on and we steamed South through Abbeville, and finally came to Amiens, there was no doubt as to our destination. From Amiens we moved on to a side line, and at 6-15 came to Flesselles, a small town about 15 miles south of Amiens, where we detrained. It was a lovely autumn evening, and with a slight breeze blowing from the East, and as we stood fallen in ready to move off from the station, we heard the low rumble and occasional growl of a big gun. From Flesselles we had to march some twelve kilometres to Rubenpre, which was to be our billeting town. Very heavily laden as we all were, officers and men, again the mistake was made of setting too fast a pace. It was an exceptionally warm evening, the men were tired, hungry and thirsty, after the long train journey, and as an hour, and then two, passed by, and we still appeared to be some distance from our town, the softer hearts in the battalion collapsed. There is no necessity to dwell on the unpleasant memories of our first route march in France; it was the most trying experience for both officers and men that we had for many a long day. As we marched East, and as the night grew darker, the flares, and the lurid flashes of gunfire became more vivid, and helped to keep up the interest of the men and distract their attention from the general weariness: at any rate we were, after eleven months' training, getting to the " Front " at last.

When we reached Rubenpré, at 11 o'clock at night, many of the men done up and all very tired, we halted at the head of the village. The second in command had gone on the previous day with the advance party to arrange the billeting, but in the darkness, of a more than usually dark night, the result of his effort was practically impossible to find. The village consisted, as far as one could judge by the light of electric torches, or matches, of a series of long barns with doors most of which were barred and bolted, and presented a remark-

RUBENPRÉ.

ably inhospitable appearance. A few days before we had left Borden we had been paraded, and in the course of a ten minutes' harangue, the Commanding Officer had dwelt upon the good name of the battalion, and its excellent conduct while in England. He told the men that he relied on them to maintain that high record in the country to which they were going. Especially he told them to respect the religious susceptibilities of the people. " Hanging over your beds in your billets you will find crucifixes, pictures of the Virgin Mary, and the Saints, and other emblems of the Roman Catholic Church and religion. You will respect these emblems, and remember that you and your Allies have come to free these people from the Germans." So throughout that march from Flesselles to Rubenpré, the men had before them the vision and anticipation of feather beds which all the saints in the catalogue might adorn, so long as it was a bed. No such luck, however, as feather beds could be hoped for in the land which the men had already christened " No man's land." So dark was the night, and so impossible to find were the billets allotted to each Company, that after nearly half-an-hour's halt at the entrance to the village, Company Commanders and Officers took the matter into their own hands, threw off their packs and equipment on the side of the street, and led their worn-out men down the village. They burst open the doors of barns, and put in, here 20, there 30, men, despite the irate remonstrances of the owners, often punctuated by some shrill scream from some female proprietor, who thought that at any rate her last hour had come. At length, on straw and hay, on floors hard and soft, everyone found a bed, and, tired, as they were, one or two were heard to mutter, Orangemen though they might be, that they wouldn't mind a bed even if the picture of the Pope himself hung at the head. In this part of France there are no farms. The country is dotted at intervals of a kilometre or two with villages, some small, some large, mostly the same in appearance, with their orchards, and grey church spires sticking up above the knots of trees. All round these villages the country stretches away in gently rolling plains, like a

great checkerboard, no ditches or hedges, reminding one
of what England must have looked like in the days of
the "common field" system. This part of the country
is intensely cultivated, not an inch of land is allowed
to go to waste, and in war time the work is done entirely
by young girls and old women. A young man was never
seen, either in the fields or villages; there seemed to be
few old men, and the small boys spend most of their day
at school. These Picard villages are intensely dirty,
and Rubenpre was even dirtier than most of them. The
barns were in a bad state of repair, and the yards were
swimming with filthy water from the great heaps of
manure which were piled up in front of each house, often
right up against the windows, yet, curiously enough, the
houses themselves were in most cases neat and clean,
The houses are built of laths, plastered with mud and
straw, poor in construction, and, owing to lack of men,
in many cases whole villages presented a dilapidated and
tumbled-down appearance. Rubenpré was, therefore,
an inhospitable place, and the reception we received
from the people themselves was not what we expected.
We felt that we had come to the country to fight for the
people, and to free them from the enemy ; in other
words we looked upon ourselves in a mild way as deliver-
ers, and felt to a small extent that we were entitled to
be received as such. But our eyes were soon opened,—
those bolted barns and inhospitable entrances were an
index of the regard in which the people held us ; we were
received with suspicion, and often with dislike, in every
village to which we came during our long peregrinations
in Picardy. It speaks volumes for our men to be able to
say, as we can say with truth, that we always went away
with the good wishes and blessings of the people, and
there were many in the battalion who, when a day off
came, would walk eight or ten miles to revisit some of
their French friends. It was only after we had been
some time in the country that we discovered the reason
for this coldness. Robbed first of all by the Germans,
they had endured successive invasions of Zouave,
English, Scotch, and Indian troops, and now an Irish
Division, a form of terror formerly unknown was thrust

upon them in its entirety. We saw that there was a certain amount to be said for their apparent inhospitality, and put up with it.

The first couple of days at Rubenpré were devoted to "shaking down." As far as my Company was concerned, we were, on the whole, fortunate with regard to our billets. There was at first a lack of straw, but this was soon remedied, and the men very soon accustomed themselves to the novelty of their surroundings. Large fatigue parties were put on from each Company, and within a week the town was cleaner than it had been for many a long day. The people looked on with quiet amusement, but they too soon became resigned to what they considered the British mania for cleaning.

Battalion headquarters were in a cottage, and at first a battalion officers' mess was tried in an estaminet which had a room in which a stove was riveted in the centre. In a short time, however, the difficulty of running a four company and headquarters mess in the same house became apparent, and two companies, A and B, seceded and formed a mess of their own in another café. C Company and headquarters remained in the same house, but before we had been many weeks in France the advantages of company messes became evident. Our company headquarters was in a disused and rather tumbled down house, but it had a good orchard and field behind, which we used for musketry and range-finding. In return for the use of the house, we lent the owner a few men every day as a help to thresh his corn and milk his cows. There was no lack of fresh milk, eggs, potatoes, and apples. Eggs cost three sous each, milk four sous per litre.

We remained at Rubenprê for about two weeks, and during that time had the usual routine of parades and training as at home. We were inspected by the G.O.C. Third Army, Sir Charles Munro, who expressed himself very pleased with our bearing on parade. We had two or three brigade field days and one divisional day, the latter the first divisional exercise under the eyes of our new G.O.C. Division, General Nugent. The remarks of our General on the day's performance were, to say the least of them, hardly as complimentary as we should have wished. They left an impression on the minds of those who heard them that will never fade, and they had their effect on all ranks.

On 18th October we left Rubenpré to go up to the line for that instruction period which everyone in the New Army in France knows so well. As we got nearer to the line the sound of the guns became more distinct, and the tiny puffs of white smoke in the sky from the German aircraft guns was the first sign of the nearness of the trenches. The country was just the same as at Rubenpre, every inch cultivated. At Varennes we were met by a band of the South Lancs., and played through the town and along the road as far as Forceville. Here we halted in a field for dinners. After dinners we fell in, and marched off by companies at ten minutes' interval, for we were now within the zone of artillery fire, being about 3½ miles from the trenches. It was only when we left Forceville that we saw any change in the aspect of the country. We now passed several lines of heavily wired trenches, which made long, white streaks across the otherwise brown and regular landscape. In other respects there were the same signs of intensive agriculture as far behind the line. We reached, at length, Mailly-Maillet, which was to be our billeting town during the instructional period. In peace time Mailly-Maillet had evidently been a very pretty little town of about 1,000 to 1,500 inhabitants, considerably better built and evidently much more prosperous than any of the villages we had seen since we came to France. There was a chateau with a fine avenue of elms which had its entrance on one side of the main street. The chateau was a Brigade Headquarters, while the avenue of elms was used as a park for transport, and was crowded with limbers and G.S. waggons up to the axles in mud. There was not a pane of glass to be seen in any of the houses; many were without doors, and some were pierced by great shell holes. Generally Mailly-Maillet had a dejected and war-worn appearance. A battery of howitzers close by caused all the window-frames in the place to shake, and every now and then a

MAILLY-MAILLET.

MAILLY-MAILLET SUCRIER

few slates would come tumbling down. As the town was full of troops, and we were an additional battalion, our billets were very poor. The men were in a very bad outhouse with little straw, while C Company Head quarters was an empty room with a tile floor in an extremely rickety condition. The first few days in Mailly were devoted to working parties. A Company was attached to the 1st Batt. Essex Regt., B Company to the 8th South Lancs., and C to the 1st Batt. King's Own Royal Lancaster Regiment, and D Company to the 2nd Royal Lancaster Fusiliers; all belonging to the 12th Brigade of the 4th Division.

The more or less eventful period of instruction which C Company experienced with the King's Own began on the night of 19th October, when No. 11 and 12 platoons working at the second line trenches on the Mailly-Serre Road, were fired on by a machine gun. It was the christening. On the 21st we paraded at 5-30 a.m., and with guides from the King's Own supplied to each platoon, marched to the trenches by platoons at five minutes' interval. The front held by the King's Own ran from the Serre Road on the right to slightly below and to the left of La Ligny farm. On our left was the Essex Regiment, while on our right were the Lancs. Fusiliers. No. 12 platoon was attached to A Company of the King's Own on the right of the Batt. line; No. 10 was attached to C Company in the centre; No. 11 to B Company on the left, and No. 9 to D company in reserve. I was with B Company on the left with Vance. The line held by the 12th Brigade formed part of the trenches taken from the Germans by the French in the preceding June. These trenches, known as the "Toutvent" trenches, had been subjected to a prolonged bombardment by the French. The latter would cease firing at intervals, during which the Germans would man the front line, and on the bombardment recommencing would retire to their dug-outs. This sort of thing went on for over a fortnight, and finally, one morning, the Germans got tired of coming out of their dugouts when the bombardment stopped, and the French swept down from their trenches behind La Ligny

IN TRAINING BEHIND THE LINES.

farm, and caught them. The victorious French advanced as far as the village of Serre, but had to fall back in the face of a terrific German counter attack, and eventually took up their position in what had been the old German second line. This trench they consolidated and held. The regiment which took the trenches was a local one, consisting of men from the region around Hebuterne, Mailly, and Bapaume. There had been reports of terrible outrages committed by the Germans on the villages behind the lines, and evidence was found in the trenches themselves to prove the truth of these reports. The story goes that little quarter was given, and the French took few prisoners, the Germans, caught like rats in a trap, being bombed in their dugouts.

B Company of the King's Own, to which I was attached, had its headquarters in a dugout known as "The Catacombs." Built by the Germans, no labour had been spared to make it shellproof and comfortable. Twenty feet deep, cut out of solid chalk, it was about twenty yards long by seven feet broad. It was divided into sections for signallers, mess, and servants' quarters, but into the wall from the mess were nooks containing beds for six officers. The whole inside of this dugout was riveted with massive planks four to six inches in thickness. There were five entrances approached by flights of steep, narrow steps. This was typical of the living dugouts in this hive of trenches. The English never built dugouts like this one in front line trenches, owing to the difficulty of getting men out of them in a hurry in case of emergency, and time after time they have proved death traps to the Germans themselves. The method of training for a battalion up for instruction is as follows:—Officers, N.C.O.'s and men are attached to their opposite numbers. Company Commander to Company Commander, Platoon Commander to Platoon Commander, sergeant to sergeant, corporal to corporal, and sentry to sentry. For three nights this proceeding is carried out, then, on the fourth night, the instructing companies withdraw to reserve, and each company takes over a sector of line on its own. Thus, bit by bit the officers and men are broken in. The first night we were in the trenches was an ideal one. A full moon made things easy, and it was quite possible to get the lie of the trenches and those of the enemy. Opposite B Company the Germans were about 100 to 120 yards away; in the centre their trenches ran to within 40 yards, and on the right about 100. There were a number of "saps" formed out of what had originally been old German communication trenches. Sand bag barricades built by each side in these formed the "sap heads." In one "sap" these barricades were about 15 feet from each other.

One may forget the incidents of one's first night in the trenches, but one never forgets the first dawn. Gradually, out of the darkness, things begin to take upon themselves their proper shapes. The first impression is that of desolation, for there is nothing so utterly forsaken or forlorn as "No man's land" at first grey dawn. A maze of misty barbed wire, some in loose coils lying on the ground, some draped from stumps and stakes driven in at all angles, some in shell holes, all in a shapeless and indescribable jumble, stretches for about three yards in depth in front of the parapet. Then there is that desolate and shell-pocketed strip of land which terminates with the German wire, and beyond that again great heaps of chalk and brown earth begin to appear as the daylight comes. These are the German trenches, and behind them is the rolling country out of which the sun now begins to rise; country that is in the hands of the Germans, away beyond the pale. Those coils of rusty wire, hung on the rickety posts, form the boundary of civilization.

The 22nd of October promised to be the most lovely day. Except for the usual amount of desultory rifle and machine-gun fire at "stand to," there was nothing to show that the Germans were about to depart from the normal state of inactivity that characterised the warfare on this sector of the front. About 8 a.m. a corporal of the King's Own " who had been doing observation work reported that the Germans had removed all their own wire, with the exception of a few strands, on their front opposite the sector held by C and

B Companies. This Captain Woodgate, commanding B Company, confirmed himself. In the " Comic Cuts," or Corps' Summary, of the previous day it was noted that the enemy had also removed his wire opposite the line held by the French, north of Hebuterne. The natural conclusion was, therefore, that he was going to attack. The state of the wire in front of our own trenches was wretched. A month before, during the period of fighting in Champagne and the battle of Loos, the wire all along the front had been removed in readiness for a possible advance, and little trouble had been taken to replace it afterwards. At 9-35 a.m., Woodgate, Vance, Brown (one of Woodgate's subalterns), and myself were having breakfast in the " Catacomb." Suddenly—" whiz-bang, whiz-bang " right at the door of the dugout. The blast from the shells knocked the cups and plates off the table. There was a pause for a second, then a terrific explosion which shook the whole earth. In half a minute we had on our equipment, and Woodgate, followed by myself, Brown, and Vance, ran up the stairs of the dug-out. The air was full of dust, and the ground in front of us seemed to be in a blaze of bursting shells. " This way," called Woodgate, and following him we ran down a communication trench leading to the front line. We had only gone a few yards when we ran into a man rushing back, blood pouring from his shoulder and arm. Woodgate stopped and caught hold of him, calling to us to run on. We ran down the trench, bending low, for a hail of shells was passing us and bursting on all sides. In a few seconds Woodgate caught us up again. I led, then Brown, Woodgate, and Vance. Suddenly, just round a curve in the trench, and about ten yards in front of me, there was a terrific explosion. I was lifted clean off my feet into the air, and thrown flat on my stomach on the ground. Almost simultaneously another shell hit the top of the trench, and before I could think where I was, or recover my breath, the whole side of the trench leant over, and fell on top of me. It was a wonderful sensation, and I remember saying to myself aloud : " I wonder when this is going to stop." Still the earth kept

falling, and the weight on my shoulders and the small
of my back became oppressive. One thing was pleasing,
there was dead silence under ground. I began to
heave with my shoulders, and took a deep breath. There
was no difficulty in breathing as the earth seemed full
of air. On the second heave I felt I was able to move,
and after what seemed ages I got my head and shoulders
clear. I was firmly fixed from my waist down, but in
less than a minute had dragged myself out. I looked
round, and saw that the entire trench had been filled in.
There was no sign of any of the others, but a small bit
of British warm coat was sticking out of the hole where
I had been which represented Brown. I got hold of it
and pulled hard. Gradually Brown emerged, cursing
like a trooper, and spitting clay out of his mouth. With
little difficulty we got Woodgate out, and Vance appeared behind him. We then ran on, and when we
came to the fire trench Woodgate called out : " Get the
men out of the living trench into the front line." The
living trench was one running just behind and parallel
to the fire trench. In it were a large number of what
were called " funk holes," scooped out of the front of
the trench, in which the men slept when off duty.
Leading from each company in the fire trench there was
a passage to the living trench. It should be explained
that by day the minimum number of men possible are
on duty in the fire trench. Sentry duty is most exhaust-
ing work, and it is possible for one man by day to suffice
where it would take ten or even twenty men by night.
In a company frontage of perhaps 500 to 600 yards
three sentries, one to each platoon would be ample in
the firing line provided there was a clear field of view to
the front ; but of course it is entirely a matter of situation and the nature of the ground. Woodgate
called to me " You take the two centre platoons and get
everyone into the trench as quickly as possible." I
ran along the living trench rousing the men, who despite the terrific din of bursting shells were mostly sound
asleep, and telling them to get out. Shells were falling
mostly in the living trench and just behind it, and I had
to go round by way of the fire trench as the passage

ONE OF THE SERGEANTS OF "C" COMPANY
IN THE TRENCHES

IN THE TRENCHES.

behind was blocked up. Meanwhile the air was thick
with flying debris of every kind—posts, iron sheets,
great baulks of timber were flying everywhere as the
enemy blew our wire to bits. In particular I watched
with fascination, a sheet of corrugated iron, blown from
the roof of a dug-out, which flew about in the air like a
card, and dashed hither and thither, finally coming
down with a great slant on the parados of the bay next
to where I was. It is no easy matter to wake the
sleeping soldier, and as I worked my way down the living trench I thought I would never get the men out of
the dug-outs. Here and there, however, where a bit
of trench had been blown in, men were creeping out,
pulling their rifles from under the fallen clay. At
last, after what seemed an age, they began to file into
the bays. The front trench was very narrow, deep, and
well sand-bagged, and once they had thoroughly real-
ised what was going on they knew it was the safest place.
Owing to the double number in the trenches nearly
every bay was manned by at least two men. Bayonets
were fixed, and ten rounds fixed into the magazine, and
we felt quite ready for what I expected would come any
minute. The shell fire now became terrific, and
practically the whole living line was filled in, the shells
just missing the front line and lighting on the step of
ground some ten yards inside separating it from the
living trench. Curiously enough no shells were lighting
in the fire trench. Two bays on the right of the two
platoons under my charge had been knocked in during
the first few minutes of the bombardment. They
formed a small salient, and presented a very easy target
to the enemy, whose artillery was mostly operating
from Serre wood. Once the fire trench was manned
there was little to do except go up and down the trench
and see that all was well. The stuff the Germans were
sending over was composed of every imaginable form
of ordnance. The biggest shells were probably eight
inch, and the air was thick with aerial torpedoes,
minenwerfer, and oil drums. The latter came hurling
through the air turning over and over and exploding
with a terrific crack, making a very large crater.

Aerial torpedoes, designed more for moral effect than to cause actual damage, burst with a nerve shattering explosion. I noticed that the closer one was to a bursting shell or aerial torpedo the less the noise, it was more of a sharp click, the greatest effect would be at almost 30 yards, under that the sound did not seem so great, though the concussion of course was terrific. Meanwhile the Germans, though they had blown most of our wire away showed no signs of attacking. It was just one of those small intensive bombardments known at the front as " a morning hate " or " straffe." When this had lasted about an hour and a half, our artillery began to retaliate. Those were the days when ammunition was precious, and each battery strictly limited. It was a pleasant sound, however, to hear the whiz of our own shells overhead and see a great mass of earth rise from the German lines, and this had a marvellous effect on the men. They at once became cheerful, the Lancashire men especially. " Thar goes a Lloyd George for you," as the whiz of a heavy shell like an express train overhead was heard. " Bah, he's a dud." " Say, Jock, the lassie 'as made 'im forgot to put in the vital spark." " There goes Fritz's iron rations " as a salvo of shrapnel burst over the first line. On the whole, however, our artillery retaliation was poor.

About 11-30 the bombardment began to die down, and by 12-30 it was over. The damage done, considering the number of shells fired into such a small sector was very small. Two bays on the right of " B " Company were completely flattened, otherwise there was no damage done to the fire trench. The living trench and communication trenches suffered more. Two of the latter had been knocked in, while the living trench along the company line had been badly battered. One very gruesome effect was noticed. There were a large number of Frenchman's graves in the parapet of the fire trench, for the French have a habit of burying a man where he falls, whether at his post or not. A hole was opened in the side of the trench, the body was shoved in, and the grave filled up. A little cross surmounted by the dead man's cap, and often his bayonet and rifle, marking the spot. In places where the fire trench had been hit or shaken many of the remains stuck out, and in many cases buttons and badges were "souveneered" by the men.

When the bombardment was over Woodgate told me it was the most severe they had experienced since May 8th, at Ypres, and quite an unusual occurrence on that front. Two men were killed and sixteen wounded, very small casualties taking into consideration the intensity of the fire. That night we dug a new trench behind the small sector blown in. There was a full moon, and walking about on top was very interesting. The ground was honeycombed with shell holes, while in all directions unexploded shells were lying about. A trench which had been used by the French for the purpose of burying dead had been unearthed in many places and the ground was littered with old equipment, clothes, and bones. I remember thinking it was the most appalling refuse heap I had ever seen. Next day was very quiet, we began work on the new trench at about 7-30, and I took charge of the three working parties in it. A considerable amount of work had been done the night before, and only a short piece remained to be dug in the centre. At 8-55 I told the men to take a ten minutes "easy" and went up to the left platoon to see one of the Sergeants about rations. I had gone about five minutes when a salvo of "whiz bangs" (77 mm shells) burst right in the trench where the men had been working, and immediately afterwards very heavy rifle fire broke out on our right. The "stand to" was passed down and the rifle fire went on for about half-an-hour, especially in the direction of "C" Company. All had quieted down about 10 o'clock. I then ascertained that a party of Germans had endeavoured to bomb "C" Company's trenches. A very large number of bombs were thrown, and in all sixteen men were wounded. For their coolness in this attack our men were greatly commended, and one man, Andrew Marshall, of No. 11 platoon, was specially recommended for devotion to duty. Badly wounded in the hand, and unable to use his rifle, he refused to leave the trench, and kept loading rifles for the men on the fire step.

The remainder of our time in the trenches was very quiet. On Sunday, 24th October, we took over the line held by " A " Company King's Own as a Company the King's Own going back into support, and the following evening we marched back to our billets in Mailly-Maillet. Our period of instruction had been most useful, for " C " Company in particular. We had experienced a bombardment and a bomb attack in both of which the men had proved their metal, and shown what was in them. As far as the Officers of " C " Company were concerned, those who came in contact with Capt. Woodgate will never forget the lesson they learned from him. " A " and " B " Companies attached to the Essex and South Lancs. Regiments had a quiet time, but " D " Company attached to the Lancs. Fusiliers in the Redan salient had their initiation into mine warfare, a platoon being in the salient when the Germans blew up a mine without, however, causing any loss of life. A good story is here told of Lieutenant W. He was out one night with a small patrol, the pass word being "Shakespeare." A large German patrol was sighted and W and his patrol had to retire in some haste. W himself fell headlong into a sap on the top of the astonished sentries with the ejaculation "For God's sake let's in, Shakespeare."

We left Mailly early in the morning of October 26th, and marched down through Forceville and Varennes to Puchvillers where we stayed the night. Next day we marched to Fienvillers and went into billets. Fienvillers was a better town than Rubenpre. There were better barns for the men, and for a company headquarters mess we were lucky to get a lovely house standing in its own grounds with bedrooms for each Officer. We now had heard our fate, it was that the 107th Brigade was to go up to the trenches to take the place of the 12th Brigade of the 4th Division, which was coming out and going to be attached to our Division. Our two remaining Brigades were to be in Army reserve for about three months. Our Battalion, with the 14th R.I.R. from the 109th Brigade, was attached to the 12th Brigade under General Auley, taking the

FIENVILLERS

FIENVILLERS.

places of the Essex Regiment attached to the 109th
Brigade, and Lancashire Fusiliers attached to the 108th
We joined the 12th Brigade at St. Leger-les Domarts on
the 5th November, the King's Own being billeted in the
same town. We now began a new and extensive system
of training, both in march discipline and attack.
General Auley, during the first week that we were in his
Brigade gave the Officers a series of lectures on the re-
treat from Mons and the subsequent advance to the
Marne. We heard the story from his own personal
point of view, which made it a fascinating narrative
rather than a tactical lecture. During the five weeks
in which we were attached to his Brigade we obtained
much practical and useful knowledge. In march
discipline, especially, we improved greatly. We were
taught that the most men can do with comfort is 112
paces to the minute. The pace was set from the rear
and not from the head of the column. Company
Commanders riding at the rear of their Companies were
made to check the pace. The utmost importance was
paid to keeping in step, and keeping the sectors of fours
well dressed and well covered down. The rifle was
carried at the sling, never over the shoulder, the reason
for this being that men, when they get tired, will let
their butts drop, and keeping hitting the man in the
sector of fours behind, thus causing loss of space in the
section, in the Company, and so on down to the Brigade
and Division on the march. We did many long route
marches, and the General used to hide in all sorts of
weird places to watch us go past, and take us unawares.

During the time we were in St. Leger, Major Clarke
(Officer Commanding " C " Company) left the Battalion
and joined the 108th Brigade as Staff Captain. I took
over command of " C " Company on November 12th.
Our Company headquarters were in the Cure's house
the Cure, like most of his confreres in France, having
gone to the front. On 27th we moved from St. Leger
to Buigny l'Abbe, a small village about three kilometres
from St. Requier where we were billeted until December 10th. Buigny was an unhealthy low lying village,
and we experienced a considerable amount of sickness,

ST. LEGER

LIEUT. VANCE, CAPTAIN SAMUELS, LIEUT. YOUNG, LIEUT. ELLIS

" C " COMPANY, ST. LEGER.

principally influenza. Our stay of a fortnight was unpleasant, it rained most of the time, and the people were inhospitable. This, we found, was due to bad conduct on the part of a Regiment which had preceded us there. The triangular pond, which is a feature of all Picard villages, had in former days formed the fish pond of the ancient monastry of Buigny l'Abbe ; and for this reason was held in more respect by the villagers than most ponds of its kind. Unfortunately, whether by accident or design, some bombs were thrown into this pond one night, and in the morning the villagers woke up to find their pond gone, and in its place a chasm of liquid mud. On investigation it was found that the bombs had burst in what proved to be the roof of a subterranean passage leading from the monastry, and through this the water had disappeared. During our stay in the town we had working parties engaged in making good the damage.

On December 10th we rejoined the 108th Brigade, moving from Buigny l'Abbe to St. Mauguille, a faubourg of St. Requier. This proved to be the most pleasant town in which we had as yet been billeted. Two Companies " B " and " C " were in St. Mauguille at Neuville, about one mile from St. Riquier. We had excellent billets both for Officers and men, and as we had now thoroughly acquired the nack of making ourselves at home, settled down very comfortably. The people were most hospitable. There were excellent, hot and cold shower baths for the men, and a Battalion laundry was set up. For our Company Mess, Monsieur Vivien, the manager of a big phosphate works gave us the greater part of his house, and he and Madame Vivien with their daughter, did all they could to make us feel at home. St. Requier was a most interesting old town. It had successfully stood siege by Henry V. and the English on two occasions, but had been sacked and burnt by the Burgundians in the end of the 15th century. Large portions of the walls still remain, and some of the old towers. In a moated farm-house just outside the town Jeanne D'Arc spent a night on her way to her trial at Rouen. Another fact of great interest was that the ancient Abbey of St. Requier had been founded by our own countrymen in the 6th century*.

See Note, Appendix I.

TOMB OF THE FIRST IRISH SAINTS.

MONSIEUR VIVIEN AND FAMILY

C

We spent a happy Xmas at St. Requier, and as we were in billets decided to make the best of it. The men were in excellent health and spirits, football, shooting, and route marches keeping them in training. The 18th of December being "Lundy Day," was celebrated by some Derry men and other Ulster boys, the following being a description of the celebration by an Officer. "Two Lundy's had been prepared, one large and the other small. Some of the inhabitants suggested that they were father and son. The father was about eleven feet long, stuffed with straw, and with rockets put in unexpected places. He had large wooden feet and wire knees, and his head filled with gunpowder and surrounded by a large yellow trimmed hat in the shape of an Admiral's. On his chest was a placard bearing the words "Lundy the traitor." The procession, headed by torchlights and band, marched through the village playing such airs as "No Surrender," "Derry Walls" and "The Boyne Water." Lundy was then let down on a wire rope from a tree where he had been strung up, and set on fire, amidst great cheering and boohing. He was well soaked with petrol and burnt excellently. Every now and then someone gave him a shake and his knees wobbled in most realistic fashion. Bombs made of jam tins were thrown into a pond just beside him, and of course broke the windows of houses in the vicinity. The procession then reformed, and marching to the top of the village, where Lundy junior was burnt with like ceremony.

Christmas, of course, produced a series of dinners given by the Officers Commanding Companies and Battalion Headquarters. To read the menu cards it was hard to believe we were in France, and that this was the second year of the war. One particularly elaborate dinner was given on Christmas day, to which we invited Madame Vivien, our kind hostess, and her family. The following is a copy of the menu in which most of the guests are represented.

Potage Vivien.
Poulets Roti au Capitaine.

Petits pois Lieutenant.
Rosbif au Docteur.
Pommes de terre Louis (the little son).
Fruits, plumb pudding, Xmas deserts.
Cafe.
Vins—Muscatel—Bordeau—Whiskey.

TOASTS.

Le Presedent de la Republique.
Le Roi D'Angleterre.
Mesdames, Messures Vivien.
Les Allies au paix glorieuse.

A service was held in the ancient Abbey of St. Requier on Christmas Day, and a sacred concert, which gave our men an opportunity of listening to Christmas music.

An incident happened about this time at St. Requier which caused no little excitement. A French billet belonging to the Downs (13th Battalion Royal Irish Rifles) went on fire. At the sound of the fire alarm every one turned out to assist the French people who stripped to the waist were hard at work trying to save their farm. The fire was raging fiercely round the stables and out-houses, and it was quite impossible to save all the horses, some of whom were burned to death in their stalls. It was a horrible sight.

On January 8th, our Battalion moved to Bernavillers. We were now beginning to think of the trenches again, and many were the rumours. Everyone seemed to know for certain our exact peregrinations during the next few months, but in truth no one could tell from day to day what our next move would be. There were also rumours of a more pleasant character, but so far only spoken of with bated breath, the one and only hope of our existence—" Leave " had begun. Our first " leave " and all that the word means. There is no doubt of it that the first leave is the best, but your first leave you are then indeed a hero, whether from billets or trenches, and your dear people who have not yet become accustomed

THREE SERGEANTS OF "C" COMPANY.

AT ST. RIQUIER.

to those short ten days have waited and watched for it
with an intense longing and pride in their hearts ; is it
any wonder one's blood thrills with the thought of that
never-to-be-forgotten home coming.

At Bernavillers an excellent concert party was formed
by Lord Farnham, called "The Divisional Follies" or
"The Merry Mauve Melody Makers." Their first
concert was honoured by a visit from The Most Rev. Dr.
Crozier, Lord Primate of Ireland, who had come to
France on a tour among the Irish Divisions. He had
already paid a visit to the 107th Brigade, who had been
having a strenuous training in the trenches ever since
October. They had escaped with very few casualties,

My Company now got orders to move to Beauval,
where we took over billets from the Y.C.V.'s (14th
Battalion Royal Irish Rifles). They were the cleanest
billets I can remember in France, and the Y.C.V.'s
deserve great praise for the way in which they were
left for us. After a week of preparation we moved on
to Canaples, and from there to Martinsart where we
again manned the trenches, and went in alongside the
9th Inniskilling Fusiliers by Companies, "C" and "D"
Companies in front with "A" and "B" in reserve.
The next week we went into support with "D" Company, and "A" and "B" took our place in front.
This time we were not attached to a regular Battalion
for training, but took over part of the line ourselves.
Our period in the trenches was uneventful, it was a
quiet part of the line, and the trenches were deep and
well made. This time we gave the Boche 500 to every 50
of theirs, so all taken into consideration we were lucky.
The weather, however, was by no means favourable, the
trenches being full of slush and water. A heavy fall
of snow also made the ground in a bad condition, and
the men suffered greatly from the cold, which was intense. Several new Officers joined our Battalion about
this time, for which we were very thankful, as leave
was able to proceed without difficulty, two Officers being
sent each week. On February 29 our first death
occured, poor young Watt of No. 12 platoon. He was
killed by a shell while standing outside the door of his

billet in Mesnil, and buried in Mesnil Ridge Cemetery.
From this time on we went into the trenches by Battalions, alternately with the Downs (13th Royal Irish
Rifles). Our casualties were not great, but always a few,
the expected result of trench warfare. Indeed, if it
had not been for a tot of rum at " stand to " on those
very cold mornings, I feel sure there would have been
more work for the hospitals. About March 6th the
weather began to improve and we occasionally felt dry.
We now began to think about giving Jerry something
to stir him up as he seemed to have gone underground
completely during the cold weather. Evidently Battalion Headquarters also felt that the time had come
to stir for we received a message to supply a specimen
of German wire as it was wanted by the corps. The
job was given in " C " Company to Young, our scout
Officer, and four other scouts. On a dark and snowy
night they crept out on patrol, and procured a good
specimen about a yard long. The other Companies also
procured specimens and the Corps appeared satisfied
with results. Our Batteries also began to wake up,
and we kept them well informed as to the position of
the German transports, which from this time on never
got a moment of peace. The 10th Inniskillings on our
right, under command of Colonel Ross-Smyth, got a
terrific shelling from the Bosche on the night of the
10th-11th of March. Shells came over at the rate of 60
to the minute, but the 10th showed splendid coolness
and gallantry, keeping up a steady fire from the front
trenches throughout the bombardment, which was
evidently intended by the Germans to cover a raid on
our lines, similar to one which took place elsewhere the
same night. An Officer, describing the bombardment
in a letter, writes—

"The Bosche has been very prodigal of shells for a
day or two, all along the front, but particularly on the
somewhat unpleasant sector occupied by the "Derry's."
On this particular afternoon he had subjected it to a
smart bombardment with "heavies," field guns, and
trench mortars. Then he fell short and waited. At
eleven o'clock precisely he opened fire with guns of all

OFFICERS OF "C" COMPANY.

ST. LEGER.

calibres. Over the Derrys he burst shrapnel, reserving his high explosive for the Donegals and Fermanaghs, and for the Brigade on their right. Not content with peppering the line, the supports, and the reserves, he shelled half a dozen villages to the rere, with which he did not as a rule concern himself. It was a very dark night, and the flashes of the guns seemed to cut through the darkness like spear points. Before the Bosche had been firing five minutes our guns had begun to reply to him, and the eighteen pounders commenced to whiz over our heads on to their front line, and soon the men in the trenches heard the welcome whistle of a high travelling howitzer over their heads in the right direction. Then indeed the din was indescribable, so fast and furious did the game become that at one time it seemed as if the boom of the big guns, the harsher bark of the small, the explosion of the shells, and the tearing crash of bursting mortars were all blended into one continuous roar. The trenches of the "Derrys" had an ugly time of it. Dug-outs were caved in, and traverses smashed down, one whole sector of the front line being practically ploughed up. At one time the enemy proceeded to pound the flank out of one Company with high explosives for several minutes, then lifted to the opposite flank and gave it the same measure. This evidently appeared to him a satisfactory idea as he repeated the manoeuvre. But the Company Officer had by now appreciated his tactics, and by his work undoubtedly prevented a great number of casualties. Gradually the German fire on the front line slackened and ceased, though it still continued overhead, and our "heavies" now warmed up to their work showed no inclination to give up. It was at this juncture that a sentry came running back from the sap head to report that he had seen Germans moving in front of the wire. The order was given to the men to stand up on the fire step, and send bursts of rapid fire in the direction of the German line. If the raiders had intended coming over this caused them to change their minds. The "Derrys" stood to till morning, but nothing fresh occurred. Through the night the men prayed their Officers to lead

Fire Trench

Our Wire

The way they went.

The Sap.

The Listening Post.

The way they went back

150 yards

Lone Tree

Snipers Post.

Ditch Bank

The German wire found attached to box.

To the German Lines.

Where they first found the Wire.

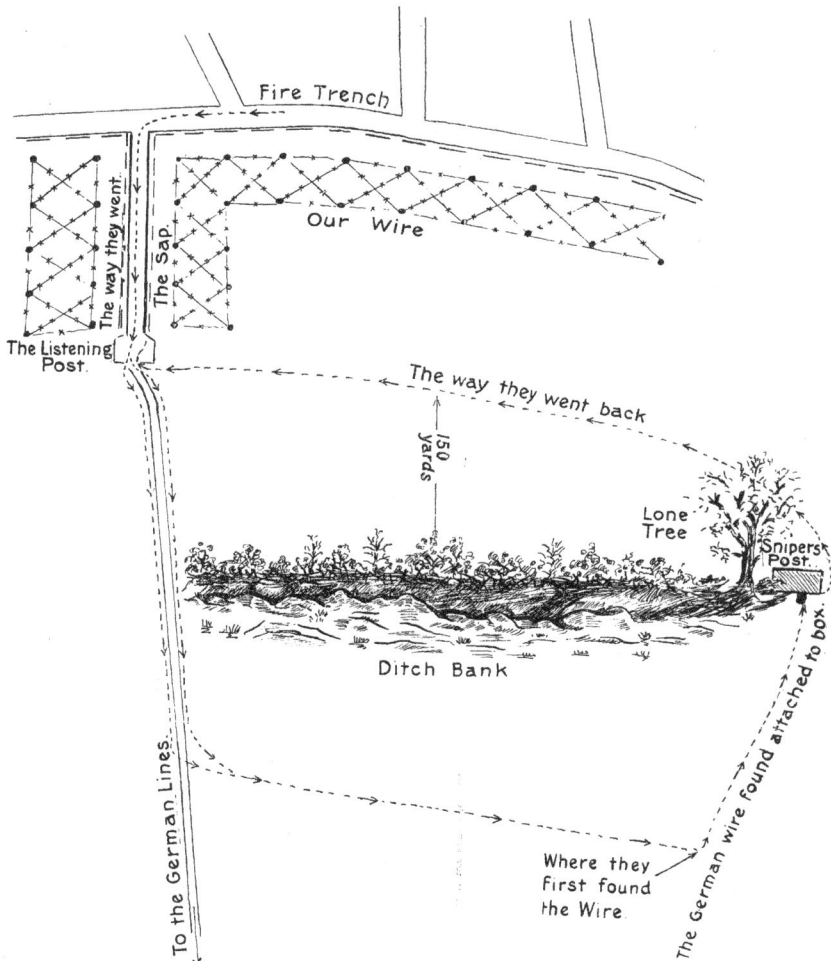

Bombs found on night patrol just in front of BEAUMONT HAMEL, March, 1916.

them over to vengeance, but for that they will have to wait. The loss was slight considering the intensity of the bombardment. When morning came the " Derrys " learned that the famous raiders had entered the trenches of the Battalion on their right, which, by the way, did not belong to the Ulster Division, and carried off an Officer and nine men as prisoners. It was a workmanlike job without a doubt, for the raiding party had come and gone within ten minutes."

Several of the men of the Inniskillings earned commendation from Colonel Ricardo for conspicuous gallantry on this occasion ; their names were Private D. Little, Private J. J. Young, Lance Corporal Black, and Private W. Dinsmore. They were serving as Company Officers, Orderlies, Signallers, and Messengers. Captain Cruickshank, of Omagh, also showed great coolness and valour on that occasion.

The weather still continued fine, and our time was spent in building new traverses, and rivetting and sandbagging the parados and firesteps. Bosche aeroplanes, taking advantage of the fine nights, crossed our lines, and green flares were sent up from the enemy to show our positions. The Germans would then send over a number of shells, and we had several casualties. Lieutenant Waring of " A " Company being hit by shrapnel, and Privates Moffat and McBride of " C " Company badly wounded. Poor Moffat subsequently died from his wounds.

We were now stirred to think of raids and night patrols. The following is an example of a patrol done by one of my Officers and some men of " C " Company. Lieutenant Young, Sergeant Renshaw, Riflemen Storey, Pollock, M'Dowell and M'Kelvey. March 16th. " C " Company Patrol Report.

" Patrol went out from Sap in Sector 41 at 7-30 p.m., consisting of one Officer, one Sergeant, and four Riflemen. On leaving our wire we turned north, striking sunken road which runs north-east in direction of German trenches. After going about 100 yards down this road we turned off under a ditch running north-west from the road. There were a number of small

THIEPVAL CHATEAU

MESNIL CHATEAU.

thorn trees on this ditch, and we could distinctly see footprints and elbow marks round them, also pits had been dug which could be used by snipers. Further along the ditch we came to a lone tree, which can be seen from Sector 49 in our lines, here we halted. About 20 yards from the tree we discovered a wire which came from the direction of the German lines. Following this we found it entered the parapet of a sniper's pit, just beneath the lone tree We then dug out the wire, and discovered it was attached to a square box covered with felt. This box we opened, thinking it contained a telephone, but instead found four German grenades with the detonators attached to the wire. We quickly disconnected the wire, and dug out the box. Not far from the spot we found another German grenade which we also took with us. At 10 p.m. we returned to our own trenches. A working party of the enemy could be heard, but it was difficult to say from which direction the sound came. Otherwise everything was normal."

G. O. Young, Lieutenant.

On March 18th we went into reserve, and were billeted in Englebelmer, being relieved on 24th by the 13th Royal Irish Rifles (The Downs). This time the 11th Battalion East Yorks were attached to us for instruction. They saw a fair amount of shelling for their first period in the trenches, the Germans putting a lot of trench mortars over on Thiepval hill. All that remained of the Chateau at Thiepval being the walls, about as high as the hall door, and a few holes where windows once had been, in all about 7ft. high by 20ft. long. The German trenches lay in front of it, on the carriage drive, and ours right up to the other side of the avenue, almost into them. Not a pleasant place, with an active sniper in the Chateau. Our trenches also ran through Thiepval wood, in which the trees were now thick with foliage. The birds built their nests and sang merrily enough on those Spring mornings. They did not appear to mind the shelling, even a cuckoo could sometimes be heard, reminding us that winter was over "this winter of our discontent." Spring had indeed come, a time when the birds call, the trees call, all nature calls for life, while we were there to kill and to be killed. There were moments when a lull came in the busy day's work, when the monotony of trench warfare left time to think, that thoughts such as these arose. We spent Easter in billets, in Martinsart village. The 23rd of April being Easter Sunday, a general holiday was given to the Battalion. Amiens, once the capital of Picardy, was about twenty-five miles distant, a long ride, but an interesting old town, and well worth visiting. Its fortifications have been turned into Boulevards, but it still retains its old citadel, and the Cathedral of Notre Dame is indeed a masterpiece of Gothic architecture. The great straight road that leads from Amiens to the front, or Albert, is the great route nationale, running from Rouen through Amiens, Albert, Pozieres, Le Sars and Bapaume on to Mons and Valenciennes. It was on this road that the famous Gordon Bennet races took place, and a better road for riding on or motoring on, it would be hard to find. The road is lined on either side with poplar trees, and a screen used to be hung from tree to tree to hide the traffic to and from Albert. There are few trees left now, and only the barest stumps, owing to bombardment. Amiens, as a rule, was out of bounds to both Officers and men, unless they were the possessors of a pass, but on Easter Monday official permission was granted to all, and many availed themselves of the opportunity to explore the ancient town. It was a chance to see civilization again, and to dine in a restaurant. At that time Amiens had not been badly shelled, even the Bosche aeroplanes seemed to be busy elsewhere, and life went on much the same as in towns at the Base. People went about their business and pleasure with very little thought of the enemy who were comparatively few miles away. The ride back at night from Amiens was rather an interesting experience. After the first six miles the sky was lit up like sheet lightning. Then the villages all became dark, no lights to be seen, then came the halts at the different outposts, the constant flashes and rockets in the sky, awful, yet fascinating. Nearer Albert the sound of the guns became clearer, and in the distance could be seen the great

Thiepval Wood. G. Sector

Scale 1:3600

Church tower of Notre Dame de Brebieres with the leaning figure of the Virgin holding the infant Christ above her head. For over a year she had hung at an angle of 15 degees below horizontal, face downwards to the street below. The French people believed that the day the holy figures fell, would see the end of the War, and that the German shell which threw down the blessed Virgin of Brebieres would shatter the throne of the Hohenzollerns.

Our Battalion being now out of the trenches the Companies were divided among the small villages around. My Company had the luck to be billeted in Autuille, a small village on the Ancre. We were able to get plenty of amusement there between rat hunting, fishing and bathing. Captain E. and I spent several afternoons trying for trout, and sent our finest specimen to " B " Company with compliments. The Ancre at Autuil was an excellent place for fishing, and this would have been a pleasant occupation were it not for the fact that snipers found us out in a short time. The bathing place was hardly 600 yards from the German lines. On May 7th the " Tyrones " had the honour of carrying out the first raid made by the Division. The following is contained in a special order of the day issued by Major General O. S Nugent, D.S.O., Officer Commanding Division. " A raid on the German trenches was carried out at midnight on the 7th inst., by the 9th Battalion Royal Inniskilling Fusiliers, the raiding party consisting of Major W. J. Peacock, Captain J. Weir, Lieut. W. S. Furness, Sec.-Lieut. L. W. H. Stevenson, Sec.-Lieut. R. W. M'Kinley, Sec.-Lieut. J. Taylor, and 84 other ranks. The raid was completely successful and was carried out exactly as planned. Six German dug-outs. in which it is certain there were a considerable number of men, were thoroughly bombed, and a machine gun was blown up, while a lively bombing fight took place between the blocking detachments of the raiding party and the Germans. Having accomplished the purpose of the raid the party was withdrawn with the loss of one man killed and two wounded. The raid was ably organised by Major Peacock, and was

ALBERT.

RUINS OF ALBERT.

carried out by the Officers and men in accordance with plan, the discipline and determination of the party being all that could be desired. The Divisional Commander desires that his congratulations should be extended to all who took part in it.''

Brigadier-General Hickman in a special Brigade Order says—'' The arrangements and plans reflect the greatest credit on Colonel Ricardo, Major Peacock, and the Officers concerned. The whole scheme was executed with great dash and determination, with cool judgment and nerve.''

The following awards were issued—Major Peacock received the D.S.O., Sec-Lieutenant Stevenson the Military Cross, Sergeant Barker, D.C.M., and Lance-Corporal D. Armour, M.M.

At this time an important change took place in the Command of the 11th Battalion Royal Inniskilling Fusiliers. Lieutenant-Colonel W. F. Hessey was promoted to Brigadier-General, and given Command of the 110th Infantry Brigade. His place was taken by Major G. H. Brush, Second in Command of the 10th Battalion (Derry Volunteers). The following farewell Order was issued by Lieutenant-Colonel Hessey to his Battalion. "Lieutenant-Colonel Hessey wishes God Speed to all members of the 11th Inniskillings, and thanks them for the loyal support they have given him from the raising of the Battalion to this day. He leaves the Battalion with very sincere regret, but with feelings of great pride that he has had the privilege of Commanding such a fine lot of Officers, N.C.O.'s and men, and that their " esprit de corps " has made the Battalion a worthy part of the 27th Inniskilling Regiment of Foot." During the following days we spent alternate periods in and out of the trenches, with little excitement to keep our spirits up. On May 16th we again took over from the 13th Battalion Royal Irish Rifles (Downs), and this time a spell of beautiful weather favoured us and the trenches were quite dry and habitable. We had the usual machine gun fire at night, especially from the direction of Thiepval Chateau, also a large number of shrapnel shells and

THE RUINS OF ALBERT CATHEDRAL.

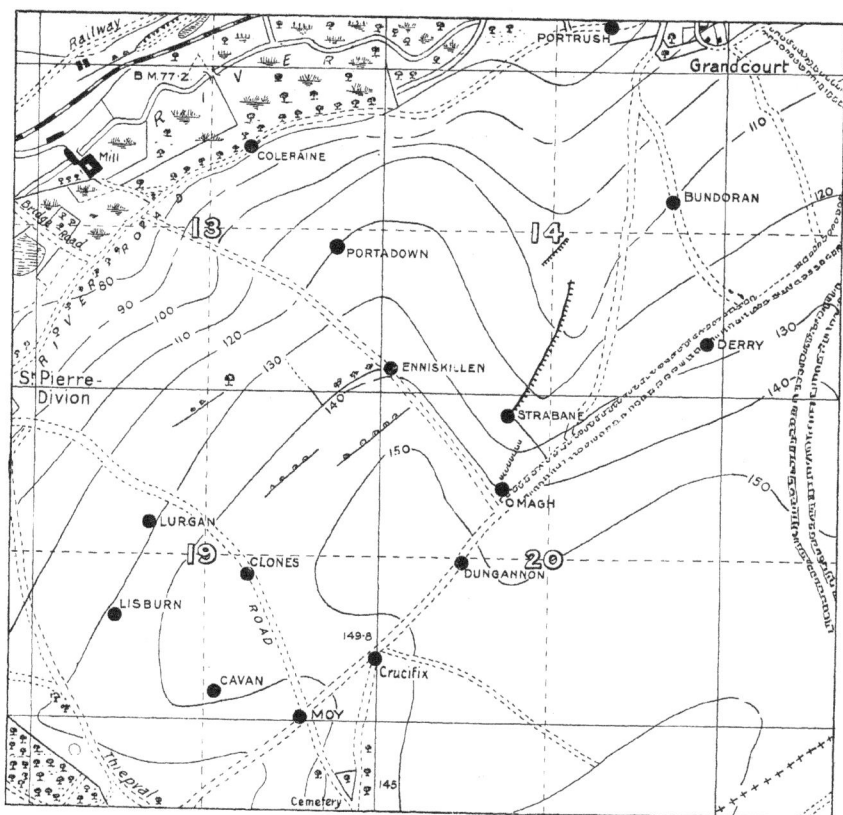

Map showing the Lines of Advance taken by Ulster Division, July, 1st, 1916.

.

whizbangs fell in our Sector. The enemy was apparently very busy during the night on his front line opposite our Company. We could hear the sound of picking and shovelling going on, and stakes being driven into the ground. During 18th-19th the enemy gave us little peace, between trench mortars, heavies, and whizbangs. Several salvoes of shrapnel managed to do considerable damage to our inspection trench and Whit Church Street. During a heavy bombardment, while the shells went over and round us at a tremendous rate I was lying flat on my stomach to avoid some shrapnel that burst near. I looked round to see if there were any casualties among the men following, and noticed a head emerging from the earth which had fallen in all round suddenly there was a splutter, the head moved, and a very solemn voice said "Boys o' boys it's aboot time the referee blew his whistle," his thoughts must have been far away on the Balmoral football ground, perhaps he was thinking of a tough fight Malone v. Queen's, in the old days.

We were glad to notice that the German trenches opposite suffered severely on the retaliation of our artillery. The following nights were busy putting up wire and sending out patrols. On one occasion a sentry reported having seen an aeroplane fall in flames some distance to the east of Thiepval, just before it fell three planes had been observed very high in the air, and the sound of machine-gun fire heard coming from them.

On the 20th there was considerable enemy machine gun activity, and a very large number of flares were sent up during the night from the German lines. At 9-30 p.m. two red flares were sent up apparently from the German salient opposite "Mary Redan." Immediately afterwards two salvoes of shrapnel were fired, and appeared to burst in the neighbourhood of "Mary Redan," while enemy search lights could be seen near Serre.

During the 21st the enemy continued his constant machine gun fire, and at night our wiring parties were much hampered on this account, one being forced to come in. At 10-30 p.m. on the 22nd, red rockets were sent up from the German lines north of the river

D

Ancre. Immediately afterwards a heavy bombardment
by enemy artillery began, apparently on our lines
in front cf Thiepval, which lasted about half-
an-hour. We had a more or less quiet day on the 23rd,
and on the 24th were relieved by the 13th Royal Irish
Rifles. "C" Company was sent to Autile, "B" to
South Antrim Villas, and the other two Companies to
Mesnil. We spent a pleasant few days in billets, the
usual rat hunts and bathing in the Ancre gave plenty of
amusement to the men. On May 31st we got our orders
to join "D" Company in Martinsart, and the following
day moved to Harponville via Bouzincourt and

THIEPVAL VILLAGE

Varrennes, where we rejoined our Brigade, and started
Divisional exercises on a large training ground known
as the Clairfaye trenches. These trenches had been
dug from aeroplane photographs, and were an exact
reproduction of the German trenches opposite Thiepval.
It was here that we heard the terrible news of the death
of Lord Kitchener, to whose genius we owed so much.
During our period of training the 107th Brigade held
the trenches at Thiepval.

On June 15th, at 3 p.m., the Battalion marched off, and with the 9th Royal Irish Fusiliers bivouacked in Martinsart Wood. Martinsart village was already occupied by numerous troops sent up in readiness for the great battle of the Somme. We sent working parties down to Thiepval wood to help in the digging of assembly trenches. Our working party was very unfortunate, and out of No. 11 platoon we had six men wounded, Miller, Lyle, Brown, Galloway. Quinn, and " B "Company also lost eleven men.

On 17th several new Officers joined the Battalion in Martinsart Wocd. among them Lieut. J. Marshall, posted to "B " Company, afterwards proved to be the only officer of the 11th Battalion who went over the top on the 1st July without getting wounded. All was bustle and excitement, we heard we were to hold the line from Thiepval Wood to La Boiselle and Fricourt.

On 22nd the Tyrones went into the trenches. We had a fine concert in " D " Company Mess, and I had a last talk to the N.C.O.'s. On 23rd we paraded at 7-45 p.m. and marched to our trenches in Thiepval Wood. Our Company Officers consisted of the following— myself, in command, Captain Ewart, Lieutenants Vance, Ellis, Young, Carson and Murphy. It was a very hot march but a glorious day, and all of us were in good heart. " C " and " D " Companies manned the front line, with " A " and " B " behind. " C " holding from Elgin Avenue to Garden Gate at the head of Cromarty Avenue. " C " Company Headquarters were in Thurso Street, and Battalion Headquarters in Cromarty Avenue. On the 26th, at 2-30, we had planned a gas attack, but there was not much wind, and the gas did not go well. Young and myself happened to be the next casualties, luckily both of us slight. Young was gassed while on duty at a gas cylinder, and I got a touch of shrapnel from a whiz bang. It meant No. 29 C.C.S. for both of us, and very reluctantly we had to leave our men just on the eve of the first and greatest battle ever fought by the Division.

PART II.

THE CHARGE OF THE ULSTER DIVISION.
ULSTER'S SACRIFICE.

Ah ! fair July of tear and sigh
Sad was the news you brought
To many an ancient noble Hall,
And humble peasants' cot,
Within our old courageous land
Of honour, truth and worth
Grave Ulster of the Iron Will,
Proud Province of the North.

H. G. Gallagher.

The following account of the great battle is taken
from different stories and official accounts given by
Officers and men who came through that memorable
day. It has been censored by several Commanding
Officers in the Division, who ascertain to the correct-
ness of it in detail. In a letter received by General
Sir George Richardson, K.C.B., commanding the Ulster
Volunteer Force, from General Nugent, commanding
the Ulster Division, the following passages occur :—

" Before you get this we shall have put the value of
the Ulster Division to the supreme test. I have no
fear of the result. I am certain no General in the Army
out here has a finer Division, fitter or keener. I am
certain they will be magnificent in attack, and we could
hardly have a date better calculated to inspire national
traditions amongst our men of the North.* It makes
me very sad to think what the price may be, but I am
quite sure the Officers and men reck nothing of that."

* General Nugent's reference is of course to the First of July, a date
sacred to Orangemen.

Our Divisional line on the right ran through Moy and Crucifix (see map), and on the left from "Mary Redan" on the other side of the river. The 109th Brigade held the line on the extreme right, 9th Inniskilling Fusiliers, and 10th Inniskilling Fusiliers in front, with 11th Inniskilling Fusiliers and 14th Royal Irish Rifles behind. Of the 108th Brigade, our Battalion was on the right nearest the 10th Inniskilling Fusiliers, then came 13th Royal Irish Rifles with 9th Royal Irish Fusiliers and the 12th Royal Irish Rifles on the extreme left. Our Battalion formed " B " and " A " Companies in front, with " D " and " C " Companies in support, " C " supporting " A " on the right, " D " supporting " B " on the left. Our object was the line marked " Omagh " "Strabane." " C " Company was to consolidate " Omagh " and " A " Company " Strabane." " D " and " B " Companies commanded by Captain Webb and Captain Craig, "Strabane " and " Enniskillen. That was as far as we had to go, which meant consolidating the 3rd German line running through " Coleraine," " Portadown," " Enniskillen," " Strabane," " Omagh." The 107th Brigade were in support behind the 108th, and we were supported by the 15th Battalion Royal Irish Rifles. The object of the 107th Brigade was then to pass through to the 4th German line, " Portrush," " Bundoran," " Derry," and consolidate it. This was as far as the Division was to go. We were to be relieved by the 49th Division when we had " done our bit." After an intense bombardment the great day of battle broke in " sunshine and mist" the mist almost obscuring the brilliant sunshine as the morning advanced. The previous night had been passed quietly in the trenches, the enemy submitting in silence to the terrific gun fire. The German lines were pulverised, shells being discharged at the rate of 140 rounds of shell per minute. In spite of this their dug-outs mostly remained uninjured. For half-an-hour it seemed as if the guns had gathered themselves together for one grand final effort before the British lines should be let loose on their prey. Presently the mist cleared away and heavy black smoke clouds could be seen drifting across the German lines on a slight south-westerly breeze, the result of the bursting of our heavy shells. This proved small assistance to us later on, when, with the sun in their faces, our men advanced from the trenches. At seven o'clock, eight of our 'planes flying over the German lines were fired at, but not much damage done. The Germans still lying low, not a single German aviator could be seen at any time that morning. Soon after 7 a.m. there was a perceptible slackening of our fire, and at 7-30 a.m. the attack began, our gallant soldiers leapt from their trenches and advanced against the enemy. The very moment that our men slipped over the parapet they were met with a hail of machine-gun bullets and shrapnel played on them. It was then that Captain Webb, of " D " Company fell, and many others. They advanced in waves 50 yards apart, and were mown down like hay. " A " Company was soon wiped out, and " C " Company, supporting it, suffered very severely; but they pressed on, gaining all their objectives. By this time there had been a severe thinning out of officers and others in command, and the men, too eager, shoved on towards the 4th line very quickly, and got into the fire of our own artillery. Some of " B " and " D " Company actually got into Grand-court. A war correspondent said: " The gallantry displayed by the carrying parties at this part of the fight was most conspicuous, and tiny escorts showed complete contempt of danger in bringing prisoners across an area which was being ploughed up by shell fire. One man, unaided, shepherded across the valley of death a party of fifteen Germans who showed extreme reluctance to risk the fire of their own guns; they wanted to lie down and wait. ' Not at all,' said the Ulsterman, covering them with his rifle, ' just you go across, and they'll look after you when you get there.'' In the course of a brief conversation several of the prisoners said that the effect of our bombardment prior to the launching of the attack had been terrific. They had been in the front lines, and while they had a reserve supply of food, our barrage fire had prevented them getting any water. Their machine-guns, they said, had been protected by being placed in deep dug-outs, and were brought up and used against our troops when they advanced.'' Within an hour and a half after the opening of the battle our men had taken five lines of German trenches and captured several hundred prisoners, advancing wave after wave like an irresistible tide. We were in advance of the Division on our left, who were to take Beaumont Hamel, and consequently the whole left flank was exposed to batteries of machine-guns: it was through this that the 12th Battalion Royal Irish Rifles suffered so severely, also the 9th Royal Irish Rifles, who supported them. '' The men advanced as if on parade; one or two remembering the ancient watchwords, sang out '' Dolly's Brae '' and '' No Surrender,'' but for the most part they kept the stiff upper lip and clenched teeth that meant death or victory. There was no thought of giving way, merely duty to be done and a task to be completed. Into the very furnace heat of the German fire our gallant lads went, and as shot and shell raked their ranks, others pressed forward to take their places. From both flanks they were enfiladed by machine-gun fire. On the right, Germans lying low in dug-outs came up from the cellars in Thiepval village with machine-guns and poured a hail of bullets into the 109th Brigade and 108th Brigade from behind. '' As they emerged from Thiepval Wood they fell in hundreds, the German fire at this point being protracted and perfect.'' The trees were slashed and cut till nothing but bare stumps remained. No one could cross that No Man's Land and escape the fire; even the wounded were shot through and through on the ground as they lay. The 107th Brigade, passing through in support to the 108th, did magnificent work. All day long the remnants of the battalions held on to the lines of the German trenches which had been captured, though nearly all the officers were gone, but no supplies of bombs or ammunition could be got across. In the evening, about six o'clock, a big German counter-attack was made, and we had to fall back, leaving our wounded, who were too bad to be moved, in dug-outs. These advanced points could not be held for long; the enemy might be killed and captured, but the place had developed into a dangerous salient, while the flanking fire from right and left made the position a terrible one, the Division on either side being held up by unsurmountable obstacles. The order to retire was given, and on Saturday night, July 1st, we were once more on our old front line. Apparently all the sacrifice had been in vain. At 1 o'clock on Sunday afternoon the remnants of the 107th Brigade and all that was left of our battalion and the 13th Royal Irish Rifles counter-attacked and easily retook the three German lines. The crucial point was the ridge that ran through "Omagh," and unless that could be held we could not hope to hold Serre and the line to La Boiselle. On the left, Beaumont Hamel commanded all, and on the right Thiepval village was the strong point. Unless these were captured our divisional line became a salient raked by machine-gun fire. The 32nd Division actually passed through Thiepval village, but the Germans, who were hidden in the cellars and concrete dug-outs, allowed them to pass, and then came up from behind, and the casualties were appalling. The 12th Royal Irish Rifles and the 9th Royal Irish Fusiliers, on our left, were practically wiped out. The Germans staked all on holding the ridge. 70 of the 15th Royal Irish Rifles and 113 of our 11th Battalion answered their names on Saturday night, and that was before the fierce fighting of Sunday. One of the most remarkable facts was the enormous number of slightly wounded men among our casualties; and as for the medical organisation, nothing could surpass it; no tribute could be great enough for the divisional medical staff. It was a magnificently heroic fight, and one of which Ulster has every reason to be proud.

THE RED HAND OF ULSTER.

Somme—July 1st, 1916.

When one great wave has shatter'd
 A coast that gleamed in light,
We look, and share the wonder,
 Amazement and affright;
But what can hide its grandeur,
 And what can veil its might?

*   *   *   *   *   *

On grey and heathy hillsides,
 In valleys bowered in leaves;
In wide and flowery meadows,
 Where peaceful sheep and beeves
Strayed thro' the days of waiting,
 No change the eye perceives.

The mist-clouds veil the mountains,
 The mist-rains drift and wing
Across the ancient castle,
 The homely cot, where cling
The climbing sprays of woodbine,
 Where wild birds hop and sing.

*   *   *   *   *   *

Now comes the news of battle—
 The long-awaited roll
Of our great Western rampant—
 A wall of thews, and soul—
And Ulster's sons are writing
 Their names upon a scroll.

That rain-swept mist-land gathers
 Before their eyes, as forth
They sweep—the watched-for Ulsters,
 For honour of the North;
For Freedom's best and dearest,
 For Britain's word and worth.

That wave of Northern valour
 Is like the advancing tide,
And nought can cool or curb it,
 And nought can change its stride;
In "Derry," "Enniskillen,"
 And Omagh they reside!

'Tis Lurgan and Dungannon,
 Armagh and proud Belfast,
St. Johnston, Londonderry,
 And Donegal's grey vast
That flit before their vision
 As trench by trench is passed.

The roar of bursting cannon
 Breaks voices faintly heard—
The voices of their youth-time,
 Familiar jest and word;
But, hark! the call is "Onward!"
 And visions grow more blurred.

    *   *   *   *   *   *

Hurrah! the drive so eager,
 So long-continued, deep,
The firmly-driven bayonet,
 The stumble and the leap
Grow less intense; the foeman
 Has wavered in the sweep!

And in the lone, grey cottage
 A trembling hand essays
To hold the fateful message
 Which speaks a proud son's praise:
" He nobly did his duty,
 And fell—there is a haze. . . . ."

Read in another homestead—
 A loftier home, now chill;—
The page tells of a soldier
 Who led his men, until
There came the hue of sunset—
 He lives in honour still.

" Dead," do you call these heroes ?
 Dead ?—who have given birth
To all that makes life living—
 To all that is of worth ;
No, never, never write it—
 This "death" is Freedom's girth !

This wounding is for homeland—
 For Britain's winsome weal—
Through all the years advancing,
 A theme for song, a peal
That swings in jubilation—
 How Ulster met the steel !

How Ulster claimed the expected,
 Already-given cheer ;
How Ulster's hand directed
 The torch which yet shall sear
The remnant of the Prussian,
 And make the future clear !

WILLIAM J. GALLAGHER.

Galdonagh, Manorcunningham,
 Co. Donegal.

10th July, 1916.

(Published by permission of the Author.)

60

PART III.

In a specially written account of the part taken in
the big advance of July 1st by the Tyrone Battalion of
the Royal Inniskilling Fusiliers, Lieut.-Col. Ricardo,
D.S.O., commander of the battalion, says:—Just now
it is a hard struggle between pride and sorrow, and
every moment the latter surges up, and it takes a
mighty effort to keep our chins up; but we shall see it
through and begin again, however hard. Out of 19
officers who went over, 12 have gone, the very best, and
all dear pals; four came back untouched, and three
wounded got back—one of these lay out for 24 hours,
and one for 48—whilst the casualties in the rank and
file were numerous. Early on the 1st July (the boys
were convinced the date had been chosen for their
especial benefit) the battle began. Every gun on both
sides fired as fast as it could, and during that din our
dear boys just walked out of the wood and up gaps we
had cut through our parapet, and out through lanes in
our wire. I shall never forget for one minute the extraordinary sight. The Derrys, on our left, were so eager
they started a few minutes before the ordered time, and
the Tyrones were not going to be left behind, and they
got going without delay—no fuss, no shouting, no
running; everything orderly, solid, and thorough, just
like the men themselves. Here and there a boy would
wave his hand to me as I shouted " good-luck " to them
through my megaphone, and all had a happy face.
Many were carrying loads. Fancy advancing against
heavy fire carrying a heavy roll of barbed wire on your
shoulders! The leading battalions suffered comparatively
little getting out, but when they came close to the
German front line they came under appalling machine-
gun fire, which obliterated whole platoons. And alas!
for us, the division on our right could not get on, and
the same happened to the division on our left, so we
came in for the concentrated fire of what would have
been spread over three divisions. But every man who

remained standing pressed on, and without officers or
N.C.O.'s they "carried on," faithful to their job. Not
a man turned back, not one. Eventually, small knots
belonging to all the battalions of the Division (except
two) gathered into the part of the German line allotted
to the Division and began to consolidate it. Major John
Peacocke, a cousin of Lady Carson, a most gallant and
dashing officer, was sent forward after the advance to
see how matters stood. He took charge, and gave to the
representatives of each unit a certain task in the
defence. The situation after the first few hours was
indeed a cruel one for the Ulster Division. There they
were, a wedge driven into the German line, only a few
hundred yards wide, and for 14 hours they bore the
brunt of the German machine-gun fire and shell fire
from the sides; and even from behind they were not
safe. The parties told off to deal with the German first
and second lines had in many cases been wiped out, and
the Germans sent parties from the flanks in behind our
boys. The Division took 800 prisoners, and could have
taken hundreds more, but could not handle them.
Major Peacocke sent back many messages by runners.
They asked for reinforcements, for water, and for
bombs, but no one had any men in reserve, and no men
were left to send across. We were told reinforcements
were at hand and to hold on, but it was difficult, I
suppose, to get fresh troops up in time. At any rate,
the help did not come. I sent off every man I had—
my own servant, my shorthand clerk, and so on—to get
water out of the river; the pipes had long before been
smashed. On their way, many, including both above-
named, were killed by shell fire. At 10-30 p.m. the
glorious band had to come back; they had reached the
third line. At 8-30 a.m. they fought to the last, and
threw their last bomb, and were so exhausted that most
of them could not speak; and shortly after they came
back, help came, and the line they had taken and held
was re-occupied without opposition, the Germans, I suppose, being as exhausted as we were. Our side eventually lost the wedge-like bit, after some days. It was
valueless, and could only be held at very heavy cost.

62

We were withdrawn late on Sunday evening, very tired
and weary. There are many instances of outstanding
gallantry, but it is almost impossible to collect evidence.
We may hear more of it when some of our wounded
come back.

A correspondent to the " Times " wrote:—

I am not an Ulsterman, but yesterday as I followed
their amazing attack I felt I would rather be an Ulsterman than anything else in the world. My position
enabled me to watch the commencement of their attack
from the wood in which they formed up, but which long
prior to the hour of assault was being overwhelmed
with shell fire, so that the trees were stripped and the
top half of the wood ceased to be anything but a slope
of bare stumps, with innumerable shell holes peppered
in the chalk. It looked as if nothing could live in the
wood, and indeed the losses were heavy before they
started, two companies of one battalion being sadly
reduced in the assembly trenches. When I saw the men
emerge through the smoke and form up as if on parade,
I could hardly believe my eyes. Then I saw them
attack, beginning at a slow walk over No Man's Land,
and then suddenly let loose as they charged over the
two front lines of the enemy's trenches, shouting " No
Surrender, boys!" The enemy's fire raked them from
the left, and machine-guns in a village enfiladed them
on the right, but battalion after battalion came out of
that awful wood as steadily as I have seen them at
Ballykinlar, Clandeboye, or Shane's Castle. The
enemy's third line was soon taken, and still the waves
went on, getting thinner and thinner, but without
hesitation. The enemy's fourth line fell before these
men, who could not be stopped. There remained the
fifth line. Representatives of the neighbouring corps
and division, who could not withhold their praise at
what they had seen, said no human man could get to it
until the flanks of the Ulster Division was cleared.
This was recognised, and the attack on the last German
line was countermanded. The order arrived too late,
or perhaps the Ulstermen, who were commemorating the

anniversary of the Boyne, would not be denied, but pressed on. I could see only a small portion of this advance, but could watch our men work forward, seeming to escape the shell fire by a miracle, and I saw parties of them, now much reduced indeed, enter the fifth line of the German trenches, our final objective. It could not be held, as the Division had advanced into a narrow salient. The Corps on our right and left had been unable to advance, so that the Ulstermen were the target of the concentrated hostile guns and machine-guns behind and on both flanks, though the enemy in front were vanquished and retreating. The order to retire was given, but some preferred to die on the ground they had won so hardly. As I write, they still hold the German two first lines, and occasionally batches of German prisoners are passed back over the deadly zone; over 500 have arrived, but the Ulstermen took many more, who did not survive the fire of their own German guns. My pen cannot describe adequately the hundreds of heroic acts that I witnessed, nor how yesterday a relieving force was organised of men who had already been fighting for 36 hours to carry ammunition and water to the gallant garrison still holding on.

The following letter sent to the "Times," July 3rd, is a description of the great day by a senior officer:—
The 1st of July should for all time have a double meaning for Ulstermen. The attack carried out by the Ulster Division was the finest thing the new armies have done in this war. Observers from outside the Division who saw it say it was a superb example of discipline and courage. We had to come through a wood which was being literally blown to pieces, form up in successive lines outside of it under a devastating fire, and then advance across the open for 400 yards to the German first line trenches. It was done as if it was a parade movement on the barrack square. The losses were formidable before we ever reached the first line, but the men never faltered, and finally rushed the first line, cheering and shouting, " Boyne " and " No Surrender !" From then onwards they never checked or wavered until they reached the fifth line of German trenches, which

was the limit of the objective laid down for us. They captured and brought in many hundred prisoners, and actually captured many more who were either killed by the German fire before they reached our lines, or were able to get away in the maze of trenches owing to the escort being knocked over. I can hardly bring myself to think or write of it. It was magnificent—beyond description. Officers led their men with a gallantry to which I cannot do justice, and the men followed them with equal gallantry; and when the officers went down, the men went on alone. The Division was raked by machine-gun and shell fire from in front and from both flanks, and our losses have been very severe.

Ulster should be very proud of her sons.

65

PART IV.

Messages of tribute to the Ulster Division from :—

The Corps Commander.
The Divisional Commander.
The Commanding Officer of the Ulster Volunteer
  Force.
Sir E. Carson.
The Lord Primate.
The Bishop of Down.
The Bishop of Clogher.
Belfast.

Lieut.-General Sir T. L. N. Morland, K.C.B., D.S.O., commanding the Army Corps in which the Ulster Division was serving, has issued the following order :—

The General Officer Commanding the Corps wishes to express to the General Officer of the Division and all ranks his admiration of the dash and gallantry with which the attack was carried out, and which attained a large measure of success under very unfavourable conditions. He regrets the heavy and unavoidable losses sustained, and feels sure that after a period of rest the Division will be ready to respond to any call made upon it.

G. WEBB,
Brigadier-General, D.A. and Q.M.G.

The General Officer Commanding the Ulster Division has issued the following special order :—

The General Officer Commanding the Ulster Division desires that the Division should know that in his opinion nothing finer has been done in the war than the attack by the Ulster Division on July 1st. The leading of the company officers, the discipline and courage

E

shown by all ranks of the Division will stand out in the
future history of the war as an example of what good
troops, well led, are capable of accomplishing. None
but troops of the best quality could have faced the fire
which was brought to bear on them, and the losses
suffered during the advance. Nothing could have been
finer than the steadiness and discipline shown by every
battalion, not only in forming up outside its own
trenches, but in advancing under severe enfilading fire.
The advance across the open to the German line was
carried out with the steadiness of a parade movement
under a fire from front and flanks which could only
have been faced by troops of the highest quality. The
fact that the objects of the attack on one side were not
obtained is no reflection on the battalions which were
entrusted with the task. They did all that men could
do, and in common with every battalion in the Division,
showed the most conspicuous courage and devotion. On
the other side the Division carried out every portion of
its allotted task in spite of the heaviest losses. It captured nearly 600 prisoners, and carried its advance
triumphantly to the limits of the objective laid down.
There is nothing in the operations carried out by the
Ulster Division on July 1st that will not be a source of
pride to all Ulstermen. The Division has been highly
tried, and has emerged from the ordeal with unstained
honour, having fulfilled in every particular the great
expectations formed of it. Tales of individual and
collective heroism on the part of officers and men come
in from every side, too numerous to mention, but all
showing that the standard of gallantry and devotion
attained is one that may be equalled but is never likely
to be surpassed. The General Officer Commanding the
Division deeply regrets the heavy losses of officers and
men. He is proud beyond description, as every officer
and man in the Division may well be, of the magnificent
example of sublime courage and discipline which the
Ulster Division has given to the Army. Ulster has
every reason to be proud of the men she has given to the
service of our country. Though many of our best men
have gone, the spirit which animated them remains in
the Division, and will never die.

The following orders of the day have been issued by General Sir George Richardson, K.C.B., G.O.C., Ulster Volunteer Force:—

1. The General Officer Commanding wishes to take this opportunity of recording an appreciation of the gallantry of the officers and men of the Ulster Division. Perhaps it may serve as a solace to those on whom will fall the heaviest burden of sorrow, and that it will help to sustain them in the knowledge that duty was nobly done, and that the great warm heart of Ulster goes out to them in affectionate sympathy and takes an unfathomable and unforgettable pride in every man of them.

2. Perhaps more especially the officers and men U.V.F. offer their heartfelt sympathy to the relatives of those who fell on the 1st July, 1916. They were put to the supreme test, and history will claim its own record.

3. For those who fell in the service of their King, the Empire, and the glory of Ulster, we mourn, but we have no regrets. We are proud of our comrades. Our path of duty is clear. Every effort must be made to fill up the casualties in the Division, and maintain the glorious lead given by the brave men of Ulster.

4. The attack of this Division is already talked of outside the Division as a superb example of what discipline, good leading and magnificent spirit can make men capable of performing. Much was expected of the Ulster Division, and nobly they have fulfilled expectation.

5. I will quote from a letter received:—" There was never a sign of falter. On the right two battalions of the 108th, the 109th and the 107th swept over four successive lines of German trenches, capturing nearly 600 prisoners and reaching the objective laid down for them absolutely on the stroke of the hour fixed as the time they might be expected to get there. On the left the 12th Royal Irish Rifles made a magnificent effort, but were swept away by machine-gun fire. They did all that men could do. The 9th Royal Irish Rifles went to them, and succeeded in getting into the German trenches, and were held up there by weight of munition and machine-guns.''

6. It fills me with pride to think how splendidly our men were capable of performing.

7. On the 30th September, 1915, His Majesty the King was graciously pleased to say to the Ulster Division:—"I am confident that in the field you will nobly uphold the traditions of the fine regiments whose name you bear." This mandate has been faithfully obeyed with a heroism and devotion that will establish a rich record in the annals of the British Army, and conveyed to us by the war cry of Ulster—"No Surrender."

GEO. RICHARDSON,
Lt.-General, G.O.C., U.V.F.

Sir E. Carson has issued the following message to the Ulster people:—

I desire to express, on my own behalf and that of my colleagues from Ulster, the pride and admiration with which we have learnt of the unparalleled acts of heroism and bravery which were carried out by the Ulster Division in the great offensive movement on July 1st.

From all accounts that we have received they have made the supreme sacrifice for the Empire of which they were so proud, with a courage, coolness, and determination, in the face of the most trying difficulties, which has upheld the great tradition of the British Army. Our feelings are, of course, mingled with sorrow and sadness at the loss of so many men who were to us personal friends and comrades; but we believe that the spirit of their race will at a time of such grief and anxiety sustain those who mourn their loss and set an example to others to follow in their footsteps.

His Grace the Lord Primate of All Ireland, who was in Dungannon holding a visitation of the clergy of the rural deaneries of Dungannon, Aghalo, and Tullyhogue, has given us the following message to the people of Ulster:—

All Ireland is proud of the noble gallantry of the Ulster Division. I have lived amongst these officers and men for the greater part of my life, and I expected nothing else. They are of the stock from which our heroes come and to whom our Empire owes so much—unconquered and unconquerable.

To-day our hearts are bowed with woe for their relatives at home who have been so grievously bereaved. For many years to come the gallantry of these sons of Ulster will be an inspiration to fresh generations of Irishmen.

I spent a considerable time with them last January in France, and I can testify to their patience and pluck, as well as to their chivalry and courtesy. Oh! the wild charge they made! Their services for honour and truth, after they have passed on into the near presence of God, will never be forgotten.

The Right Rev. Dr. D'Arcy, the Bishop of Down, in a message, says :—

The 1st of July will for all the future be remembered as the most glorious in the annals of Ulster. Terrible indeed are the losses sustained. Many of our noblest and best young men, to whom we looked for help and leadership in the time to come, have given their lives in the service of their country and for the welfare of humanity. But our deep sorrow is permeated by the sense of the joyful exultation at their splendid heroism. They have proved themselves worthy of the grandest traditions of their race. They have, indeed, surpassed all records of ancient chivalry. Wherever Ulstermen go they will carry with them something of the glory of the great achievement of the 1st July. The spirit of willing sacrifice for the sake of those great ideals of liberty and progressive humanity which belonged to all that is best in the British race, and which has inspired Ulster throughout all her recent struggles, was never more magnificently exhibited.

The Right Rev. Dr. Day, the Bishop of Clogher, writes :—

I most heartily join with the Lord Primate, the Bishop of Down and others in offering my congratula-

tions to the Ulster Division on the record of their noble
deeds at the front in taking a prominent part in the
great offensive which was begun on July 1st by the
united forces of France and England. While we regret
the heavy roll of casualties with which their great
achievements were carried out, and sincerely sympathise
with the sorrowing relatives of those who have fallen
in the cause of their King and country, the "order of
the day" issued by General Nugent is a testimony to
valour and determination which may well rouse the
admiration of everyone who is associated with Ulster.

MAURICE CLOGHER.

The following paragraph, taken from the "News-
Letter," July 12th, 1916, shows how Belfast and the
people of Ulster paid a tribute to their glorious dead :—
"This year, for the first time in the history of the
Orange Institution, the celebration of the anniversary
of the Battle of the Boyne was abandoned, while the
customary holidays were to a great extent postponed
until next month, to enable the shipyards and munition
works to complete immediate orders. At the suggestion
of the Lord Mayor, all work, business and household,
was temporarily suspended for five minutes following
the hour of noon to-day, as a tribute to the men who
have fallen in the great British offensive. Viewed from
the City Hall, on the steps of which the Lord Mayor
and Lady Mayoress were standing, the scene was most
impressive. On the stroke of 12 all traffic came to a
standstill, men raised their hats, ladies bowed their
heads, the blinds in business and private houses were
drawn, and flags were flown at half-mast. The bells at
the Assembly Hall tolled, and after the interval of five
minutes chimed the hymn 'Abide with Me.' Interces-
sory services were held in the Cathedral and other
churches. Shortly before noon the following telegram
was received by the Lord Mayor from Sir Edward and
Lady Carson :—'Our prayers and solemn thoughts will be
with you all at 12 o'clock, in memory of our illustrious
dead, who have won glory for the Empire and undying
fame for Ulster. May God bless and help their sorrowing families.'"

THE EXTERIOR OF ST. RIQUIER CATHEDRAL.

NOTE ON ST. RIQUIER.
(*Appendix I.*)

A beautiful description of St. Riquier and the
foundation of the Abbey is given in a book by Margaret
Stokes, " Three Months in the Forests of France.''

Abaut the year 589, two Irishmen, named Caidox
and Fricor, disembarked on the coast at the little town
of Quentovic, on the mouth of the Somme, with twelve
companions, and they followed the great Roman road,
now called the Chausee Brunehaut, preaching he Gospel
on their way. They reached Centule (now St. Riquier),
and remained there some days to rest. Some say they
came to France with Columban, and that when
Columban resumed his journey towards the Vosges, he
left behind him these two monks that they might give
instructions to the half-barbarous inhabitants, and
initiate them into the mysteries of the Christian religion.
" They fought on," said the old chronicler, " perceiving
that the inhabitants of Centule (St. Riquier) were
blinded by error and iniquity, and were subjected
to the most cruel slavery; they laboured with all their
strength to redeem their souls, and wash them in the
Saviour's Blood." But the people could not understand
the language of these heavenly messengers, and they
rebelled against a teaching so holy and sublime. They
demanded what these adventurers, who had just
escaped out of a barbarous island, could be in search of,
and by what right they sought to impose their laws on
them. The voice of charity was met by cries, menaces,
and outrage, and the natives strove to drive them from
their shores by violence, when suddenly a young noble,
named Riquier, appeared upon the scene. He commanded silence, and arrested the most furious amongst
the mob, and taking the two strangers under his pro-
tection, he brought them into his house. He gave them
food and drink, and in return they gave him such
nourishment of the soul as he before had never tasted.
He learned to know God and love Him beyond all
things. . . . . When he had taken orders he

THE INTERIOR OF ST RIQUIER CATHEDRAL.

became the founder of the celebrated Abbey of Centul (now St. Riquier), and the bodies of the two Irishmen from whom he had learned Christianity were interred with splendour in this church. When St. Angelbert, in the year 799, restored this church, he also restored the half-ruined tombs, decorated their shrines with such magnificence, and inscribed verses upon them in letters of gold. The relics of the two saints lay beneath the monument till the year 1070, when St. Geroinus transferred them to a silver shrine adorned with precious stones, and in this shrine also were laid the relics of another Irish saint, Mauguille. Their festival is celebrated on June 3rd. On the road from Abbeville to Doullens, on the edge of the wood of St. Riquier, and below the slope of a smiling hill, an ancient church, majestically seated in the valley below, comes into view. It is the Abbey Church of St. Riquier. The town rises from the foot of the church like an amphitheatre round the enclosure of its ancient walls. The great tower rises above the fertile fields around and above the summits of the distant hills and woodland glades. The little stream of Seardon, which almost threatens to disappear at its very source, passes through the lower town and on towards the south-west. The old chroniclers called it Reviere au Cardons, from the little flower cardoon. This little thread of water, rising at Bonnefontaine, under Isinbard's tomb, is swelled by the junction with the river Mirandeuil, or Misendeuil, a name derived from the fact that it was at this spot the ladies of St. Riquier first heard the fatal news that their husbands had fallen in the Battle of Crecy. . . . . The labours of the Irish Church in Picardy, commenced by these two missionaries, Caidox and Fricor, and carried on by the disciples of Columban from Luxeuil, were destined to receive a fresh impetus from the parent country. Another mission, this time from the shores of Lough Corrib, in Galway, was undertaken. Fursa and his twelve companions, who landed at Mayoc, at the mouth of the river Somme, A.D. 638, went up the river to St. Riquier, a monastery in which he must have found traditions of his native Church.

OFFICERS 11th BATTALION ROYAL IRISH RIFLES, July, 1915

*Top Row—*Lieut. Waring, 2nd Lieut. Ellis, 2nd Lieut. P. B. Thornely, Lieut. F. G. Hull, 2nd Lieut. D. J. Brown, Lieut. E. Vance, Lieut. R. H. Neill (Assistant Adjutant), 2nd Lieut. C. C. Canning.

*Second Row (standing)—*Lt. and Q.M. W. L. Devoto, Lieut. R. Thompson (Transport Officer), Lieut. C. F K. Ewart, 2nd Lieut. C. G. F. Waring. nd. Lieut. S. A. M'Neill, 2nd Lieut. D. S. Priestly, 2nd Lieut. W. C. Boomer, 2nd Lieut. T. H. Wilson, 2nd Lieut. G. O. Young (Scout Officer), Lieut. K. M. Moore, Lieut. M. C. Graham (Medical Officer), Captain S. D. B. Masters.

*Third Row (sitting)—*Captain Smyth, Capt. C. C. Craig, M.P.; Capt. A. P. Jenkins, Capt. R. Rivers Smyth (Brigade Major, 108th Inf. Brigade), Major P. L. K. Blair Oliphant (2nd in Command), Lt.-Col. H. A. Pakenham (Commanding), Major W. D. Deverell (Adjutant), Capt. O. B. Webb, Capt. A. F. Charley, Capt. A. P. I. Samuels.

*Two Officers sitting in front—*2nd Lieut C. H. H. Orr. 2nd Lieut. J. C. Carson.

Biographies of Officers of 11th Royal Irish Rifles (South Antrim Volunteers,) who were killed or wounded during the Battle of the Somme.

In some cases Photographs could not be obtained.

CAPTAIN C. C. CRAIG

Commanding B Company ; wounded and prisoner ; M.P. for South Antrim.

MAJOR A. P. JENKINS, Lisburn,

Commanding A Company ; wounded and prisoner ; first reported missing ; received Commission as Captain in 11th Royal Irish Rifles, September, 1914, served in France till July 1st, 1916, when wounded and made prisoner, released from Germany owing to wounds in December, 1916, spent from December, 1916, till November, 1917, as a repatriated prisoner of war in Switzerland, returned to England November, 1917.

CAPTAIN O. B WEBB,

Commanding D Company , killed in action ; son of the late Mr. Charles J. Webb, J.P., the Old Bleach Linen Company, Randalstown.

CAPTAIN A P. I. SAMUELS,

Commanding C Company ; wounded during bombardment previous to advance, afterwards killed at Messines, September, 1916 ; son of the Right Hon. Mr. Justice Samuels.

CAPTAIN E. F. SMITH,
Wounded ; son of Mr. Smith of Banbridge ; before the war was an officer in the Lisburn contingent of the U.V.F.

LIEUT. E. B. VANCE.
Died of wounds a prisoner in Germany ; C Company ; son of the late Mr. William Vance, Antrim.

CAPTAIN CECIL EWART,
Killed in action ; second in command of C Company ; he took Command of the Company after Captain Samuels was wounded. Captain Ewart is the second son of Mr. F. W. Ewart, Derryvolgie, Lisburn.

LIEUT. R. H. NEILL.
Killed ; only son of Mr. Reginald Neill, Colingrove, Dunmurry ; educated at Mourne Grange, Kilkeel, Co. Down, and Malvern College, Worcestershire. He was formerly an officer in the 2nd Batt. South Antrim Regiment, U.V.F.

LIEUT. W. ELLIS,
C Company; wounded; son of Mr. Ellis, Toomebridge.

LIEUT. G. O. YOUNG
C Company, Scout Officer; gassed in bombardment previous to advance; son of Mr George L. Young, J.P., Culdaff House, Co. Donegal, and Millmount, Randalstown.

SEC.-LIEUT. B. W. GAMBLE.
A Company; wounded; son of Mr. Baptist Gamble, 2 Elmwood Avenue, G.W.R., Belfast.

SEC.-LIEUT. G. N. HUNTER.
Wounded; second son of Mr. Samuel Hunter, Gracepark Gardens, Dublin, Public Valuer to His Majesty's Treasury in Ireland.

SEC.-LIEUT. E. DANIEL.
Shell-shock ; son of Mr Daniel,
Dungannon.

SEC.-LIEUT. J. W. SALTER.
B Company ; prisoner ; first reported
killed.

SEC.-LIEUT. C. J. H. SAMUELS.
D Company ; wounded ; nephew of the
Right Hon. Mr. Justice Samuels.

SEC.-LIEUT. F. B. THORNELY.

Wounded ; B Company ; nephew of Major
Blair Oliphant, second in Command of
the Battalion ; received his commission
from Uppingham School.

SEC.-LIEUT. J. C. CARSON.

C Company ; wounded ; only son of Mr.
J. Carson, of Parkmount, Lisburn, and
the Stock Exchange, Belfast.

SEC.-LIEUT. J. C. ORR.

Wounded ; son of Mr. J. C. Orr, London-
derry.   Was in the Hong Kong and
Shanghai Bank, London, before the war.
He was with the 108th Brigade Trench
Mortar Battery during the advance.

SEC.-LIEUT. C. R. B. MURPHY.

Wounded ; son of the Rev. Dr. Murphy,
Rector of St. George's Parish Church,
Belfast.

SEC.-LIEUT. D. S. PRIESTLY.
Killed, attached 108th Brigade Machine Gun Corps. This officer had been with D Company until January, 1916.

SEC.-LIEUT. W. C. BOOMER.
D Company, Lisburn; wounded previous to July 1st.

SEC.-LIEUT. BRAMHAL.
Wounded during bombardment previous to advance.

SEC.-LIEUT. S. WARING.
A Company, Glenavy; wounded previous to July 1st.

SEC.-LIEUT. W. P. VINT,
Wounded; was with the Machine Gun Company, 108th Brigade.

F

ORDERS No. 237.

By Lieut.-Col. H. A. Pakenham, Commanding 11th (Service) Battalion Royal Irish Rifles (South Antrim Regiment). 16th July, 1916.

313 CASUALTIES.

KILLED—1/7/16.

"A" COMPANY.

Cpl. Dunlop, Q.
L/Cpl. Lennox, F. J.
R'man. Allen, W. J.
,, Clelland, G.
,, Harvey, J.
,, Marks, R.
,, Morrow, R.
,, Leckey, W.

"B" COMPANY.

R'man. Bell, H.
,, Brown, E.
,, Gaussen, C. L.
,, Haddock, T.
Cpl. Lunn, J.
R'man. Lewis, E.
L/Cpl. M'Kechnie, R.
R'man. M'Keown, W.
,, Neill, J.
Cpl. Stewart, P. M.
L/Cpl. Walker, G. F.
R'man. Welch, Alex.

"C" COMPANY.

Sgt. Buick, J.

R'man. Andrews, J.
,, Knox, F.
,, Magill, R. D.
,, Pollock, A.
,, Wallace, J.

"D" COMPANY.

C.S.M. Bell, J.
L/Sgt. Bell, J.
L/Cpl. Foster, J. B.
,, Cathcart, T.
R'man. Ansell, J.
,, Dunleavy, J.
,, Gorman, D.
,, Hoy, S.
,, Harper, J.
,, Morrow, J.
,, M'Clean, J.
,, M'Mullen, J.
,, M'Clughan, R.
,, M'Gimpsey, J.
,, Nixon, R. W.
,, Robinson, E.
,, Smith, R.
,, Sloan, W.
,, Steadman, J.
,, Stephenson, J.
., Toman, H.
,, White, J.
,, Weir, W.

DIED FROM WOUNDS.

R'man. Boyd, D.

83

614 CASUALTIES.

WOUNDED—1/7/16.

"A" COMPANY.

Sgt. Abbott, J.
,, Patton, J.
L/Sgt. Gillespie, G.
,, Beattie, V.
L/Cpl. Atkinson, M.
,, Kerr, A.
., Lynch, E. W.
Upd.
L/Cpl. M'Neice, E.
L/Cpl. Corkin, W.
R'man. Allen, S.
,, Beck, J.
,, Bell, R.
,, Buchanan, J.
,, Barrons, A.
,, Conway, W. C.
,, Corkin, J.
,, Connaughty, R.
,, Dodds, S.
,, Frazer, R.
,, Fulton, J.
,, Hawthorne, J.
,, Hunter, R.
,, Keery, S.
,, Lavery, Jas.
,, Lavery, John
,, Lewis, G.
,, Logan, W. J.
,, Lyness, C.
,, Maginess, W.
,, Morgan, J.
,, Murdock, J.
,, Morrison, T. G.
,, Mulligan, D.
,, Mulholland, C.
,, M'Cann, E.
,, M'Cann, J.
,, Matier, R. (2)

R'man. M'Neice, J. (1)
,, Orr, W.
,, Patterson, T.
,, Reid, J. E.
,, Salley, R.
,, Sewell, F.
,, Smyth, W.
,, Spratt, S.
,, Steele, J.
,, Semple, W.
,, Savage, E.
,, Ward, T.
,, Watson, A.
,, Weir, A.
,, M'Gorkin, R.
,, Hillis, J.
,, Hanna, B.
,, Coburn, J.
,, Abbott, T.
,, Agnew, J.
,, Atkinson, T.
,, Beattie, E.
,, Cassidy, J.
,, Chapman, Jas.
,, Fox, W. J.
,, Herron, J.
,, Hanna, R.
,, Murdock, T.
,, Rainey, S.
,, Williamson, R.
,, Watson, C.
,, Beattie, R.
,, Freeland, S.

"B" COMPANY.

R'man. Benson, A.
,, Blakes, T.
,, Bleaks, W.
,, Briggs, R.
,, Bryson, S.
Sgt. Burke, F. G.

84

L/Cpl. Crawford, W. J.
R'man. Curry, W.
,, Crowe, J.
,, Crozier, W.
,, Dickson, C.
,, Dodds, J.
,, Duff, J.
,, Foreman, J.
L/Cpl. Gill, D.
R'man. Green, T.
,, Hawthorne, A.
,, Hill, S.
L/Cpl. Hull, W. J.
R'man. Hyndman, R. J.
,, Lewis, W.
,, Moore, R.
,, Mulholland, T. J.
Sgt. Munn, H.
R'man. Maybin, J.
,, Moody, T.
,, Marshall, G.
Sgt. M'Clenahan, W. J.
R'man. M'Cormick, J.
,, M'Donald, J.
,, M'Gurk, J.
,, M'Henry, J.
,, M'Knight, R.
,, M'Williams, F.
,, M'Williams, J.
,, M'Gall, J.
,, M'Cluskey, W.
,, O'Neill, J.
,, Patterson, T.
,, Ramsey, J.
L/Cpl. Rennix, E.
R'man. Scott, H.
,, Spears, D.
,, Smith, A.
,, Thompson, J.
,, Trousdale, G.
,, Verner, T.
Sgt. Waring, G. D.

R'man. Webb, H.
,, Webb, Jos.
,, Woods, J.
,, Woods, A. C.
,, Rea, S.
,, Dowling, A.
,, Matchett, J. H.

"C" COMPANY.

Sgt. Steele, M.
,, Kelly, A.
,, Whiteside, A.
,, Kernaghan, J.
L/Sgt. Swann, J.
Cpl. Fleming, H.
,, M'Burney, J.
A/Cpl. M'Burney, T.
L/Cpl. Reid, B.
,, Crookes, C. E.
,, Wallace, J.
,, O'Neill, J.
R'man. Andrews, R. J.
,, Alderdice, R.
,, Bates, R.
,, Campbell, S.
,, Cullen, W.
,, Doole, I.
,, Dawson, J.
,, Ewart, H.
,, Ewart, H.
,, Esler, R.
,, Foster, W.
,, Greer, A.
,, Gillespie, J.
,, Hamilton, J.
,, Hughes, J.
,, Hamilton, T.
,, Hanlon, A. T.
,, Harvey, J. S.
,, Hume, J.
,, Kirkpatrick, S.

R'man. Harbinson, A.
,, M'Cammond, J.
,, Linton, W.
,, Millar, J.
,, Moore, J.
,, Magill, T.
,, Milligan, J.
,, Manning, R. J.
,, M'Kee, J.
,, M'Lean, W.
,, M'Connell, J.
Upd.
L/Cpl. M'Grugan, H.
R'man. M'Clay, S.
,, M'Calmont, W. J.
,, Nicholl, S.
,, Patterson, J.
,, Sterling, D.
,, Storey, D.
,, Sergeant, T.
,, Shannan, A.
,, Stewart, J.
,, Thompson, S.
,, Thompson, J.
,, Wallace, A.
,, Woods, R.
,, Young, W.
,, Young, S.
,, Scullion, J.
L/Cpl. Eakin, T.
R'man. Bailey, W.
,, Millar, J.
,, Mulree, J.

"D" COMPANY.

Sgt. Higginson, W.
,, Mercer, J.
Cpl. Matier, T.
,, Adamson, R. M.

L/Cpl. O'Neill, E.
,, Wallace, W.
,, Shaw, J.
,, Allen, W.
R'man. Ayre, S.
,, Adair, G.
,, Adair, B.
,, Adams, K. G.
,, Allen, D.
,, Ashe, E.
,, Boomer, R.
,, Boggs, J.
,, Calvert, W.
,, Christie, J.
,, Corkin, T.
,, Cochrane, G.
,, Cunningham, D.
,, Duffy, R. J.
,, Dalton, A.
,, Doole, G.
,, Dickson, S.
,, Dawson, A.
,, Fleming, W.
,, Harbinson, R.
,, Horner, J.
,, Hill, S.
,, Johnston, W.
,, Johnston, H.
,, Kennedy, G.
,, Leathem, W.
,, Stratton, W. J.
,, Jenkins, T.
,, Lowery, J.
,, Kerr, J.
,, Lyttle, J.
,, Millar, B.
,, M'Pherson, R.
,, M'Kee, J.
,, M'Kibben, R. M.
,, M'Cloy, W.
,, M'Kibben, L.

R'man. M'Dowell, W.
,, Martin, T.
,, Mawhinney, S.
,, M'Connell, W.
,, M'Grath, J.
,, M'Ilroy, H.
,, M'Dowell, D.
,, Neeson, J.
,, Peel, A.
,, Russell, J.
,, Ringland, G.
,, Rodgers, J.
,, Steele, J.
,, Stewart, W.
,, Smyth, W. J.
,, Smith, W.
,, Shields, S.
,, Todd, J.
,, M'Clelland, S.
,, Ingram, H.

615 MISSING.

"A" COMPANY.

R'man. Chambers, J.
,, Cowan, Jos.
,, Doherty, A.
,, Davidson, J. H.
,, Emerson, D.
,, Freeland, S.
,, Kerr, D.
,, Kain, W.
,, Kidd, Jas.
,, Lightbody, J.
,, Logan, T.
,, Lyttle, S.
,, Russell, W.
,, Singleton, T.
,, Topping, S.
,, Totten, W.
,, Wright, W.
,, Kidd, R.

"B" COMPANY

R'man. Beattie, G.
,, Blakely, S.
,, Bruce, W. J.
Cpl. Cairns, E.
Sgt. Cairns, T. G.
R'man. Crowe, J.
,, Gordon, R.
,, Green, J.
,, Hawthorne, T.
,, Herron, W.
,, Henninger, W.
,, Hanna, D.
,, Irvine, W.
,, Kidd, G.
,, Kennedy, R. J.
,, Kennedy, R.
,, Logan, T.
,, Lowry, H.
,, Lyness, J.
,, Marks, T.
,, Murdock, H.
Upd.
L/Cpl. Murphy, T.
R'man. Morrow, J.
,, Morrow, R. J.
,, M'Ilhatton, R.
,, M'Larnon, G.
,, Patterson, W.
,, Reid, D.
,, Stevenson, J.
,, Semple, S.
,, Semple, S. J.
,, Tollerton, R.
,, Wills, S.

"C" COMPANY.

Sgt. Stewart, W.
,, Miller, W.
L/Cpl. Scott, J.
,, Ellis, S.

87

R'man.	Anderson, W. H.	L/Cpl.	M'Aleece, J.
,,	Bell, A.	,,	Smyth, J.
,,	Clarke, A.	,,	Robinson, W.
,,	Coulter, J.	R'man.	Bushe, S.
,,	Drennan, R.	,,	Bell, A.
,,	Dyers, J.	,,	Easton, S.
,,	Derby, G.	,,	Goudy, J.
,,	Graham, D.	,,	Heaney, T.
,,	Greer, A.	,,	Logan, W.
,,	Houston, W.	,,	Moore, H.
,,	Linton, H.	,,	M'Curdy, W.
,,	Lyttle, F.	,,	Moore, J.
,,	Marshall, A.	,,	M'Allister, J.
,,	Mairs, E.	,,	Patterson, R.
,,	M'Dowell, J.	,,	Skillen, W.
,,	M'Fall, J.	,,	Thompson, J.
,,	Newell, T.	,,	Williamson, A.
,,	Nelson, W.	,,	Wilson, T.
,,	Orr, J.	,,	Hamill, J.
,,	Smith, W. J.	,,	Graham, J.
,,	Wilkinson, W.	R'man.	Boyd, W.
		,,	Boyd, D.
		,,	Henderson, J.

" D " Company.

Upd.
L/Cpl. Millar, S.

Sgt. Lavery, G.
A/Cpl. Moore, W.
Cpl. Glendinning, D.
,, Williamson, W. J
Unpd.
L/Cpl. Purdy, R.

PRISONER OF WAR.

R'man. Fisher, J.
,, Walker, H.
,, Frouten, A.

ADJUTANT,
11th (S.) Bn. R.Ir.Rif.

Embarkation List of Officers

Embarkation List of Officers 11th Royal Irish Rifles
who left Bordon Camp for France, October, 1915.

Lieut.-Col. H. A. Pakenham,
  Commanding Officer.
Major P. Blair Oliphant.
Major Devonish Deverell,
  Adjutant.
Lieut. R. Thompson,
  Transport Officer.
Capt. Graham,
  Medical Officer.
Lieut. F. Hull.
Lieut. Devoto,
  Quartermaster.

"A" COMPANY.

Major A. P. Jenkins.
Capt. E. F. Smith.
Capt. C. Ewart.
Lieut. C. G. F. Waring.
Lieut. T. G. Thornely.
Lieut. S. Waring.

"B" COMPANY.

Captain C. C. Craig.
Captain A. T. Charley.
Lieut. R. N. Neill.
Lieut. Wilson.
Lieut. Webb.

"C" COMPANY.

Major Cavendish Clark.
Lieut. Vance.
Captain A. P. I. Samuels.
Lieut. Ellis.
Lieut. Young.
Lieut. Vint.

"D" COMPANY.

Captain O. B. Webb.
Captain Masters.
Lieut. Canning.
Lieut. Waring.
Lieut. W. C. Boomer.
Lieut. Priestly.

Embarkation List of N.C. Officers & Men.

Sgt. Abbott, James
R'man. Abbott, Thomas
,, Abbott, Wm. Robert
,, Allen, Samuel
,, Allen, Wm. John
,, Andrews, James
,, Andrews, James
,, Andrews, Thomas
,, Atkinson, Moses
,, Atkinson, Thomas
,, Adams, R.
,, Adams, John
,, Addis, David
,, Addis, Henry
,, Agnow, Edward
,, Andrews, William
,, Adams, Henry
,, Adams, James Alex.
,, Adams, Oliver
,, Allen, John
,, Anderson, Samuel A.
,, Anderson, Wm. Hy.
L/Cpl. Andrews, Robt. John
R'man. Ardery, Francis
,, Armstrong, William
,, Adair, Ben
,, Adair, George
,, Adams, Kenneth K.
,, Adams, Robert
,, Adamson, Robt. M'K.
,, Addis, James
Cpl. Addis, Wm. Hy.
R'man. Allen, William
,, Anderson, John Jos.
,, Ansell, John
,, Archer, Bertie
,, Ashe, Edward
,, Ayre, Samuel
,, Baxter, Isaac
,, Beattie, Ernest
,, Beattie, Robert
Cpl. Beattie, Victor
R'man. Beck, James
,, Bell, Robert
,, Bingham, William
L/Cpl. Black, James

R'man. Blakley, Edward Chas.
,, Boyd, David
Sgt. Breathwaite, Samuel
R'man. Brown, George
,, Brown, Isaac
,, Brown, Samuel
,, Buchanan, John
C.Q.M.S. Bullick, Edwin
L/Sgt. Bullick, Wm. Parker
R'man. Barr, David Geo.
,, Barr, John Nathaniel
,, Beattie, George
,, Beck, Hg. Hy.
,, Bell, Hy.
,, Bell, John
L/Cpl. Brown, Samuel
R'man. Benson, Albert
L/Cpl. Benson, John
R'man. Birney, Thomas
,, Black, William
,, Blakes, Thomas
,, Blakely, Alexander
,, Blakely, Samuel
,, Blakely, Thomas
,, Bleaks, William
,, Bloomfield, Sl.
,, Briggs, Robert
,, Brown, Edmund
,, Brown, George
Cpl. Brown, James
R'man. Brown, John
,, Brown, Samuel
,, Bruce, Albert E. G.
,, Bruce, William
,, Bruce, William
,, Bryans, David
,, Bryson, Samuel
L/Sgt. Burke, Fk. Geo.
R'man. Bankhead, Robt.
,, Barbour, Robt.
,, Barkley, Arthur
,, Bates, Robert
,, Beattie, Robert
,, Beattie, Robt. Jas.
,, Beattie, William
,, Beck, James

R'man. Bell, Andrew
  ,, Boyd, David
  ,, Brown, Fred Chas.
  ,, Brown, John
  ,, Brown, John
  ,, Brown, Robert
Sgt. Buick, Jackson
R'man Buick, James
  ,, Burrowes, Hy.
  ,, Barkely, James
  ,, Beggs, James
  ,, Bell, Andrew
  ,, Bell, Alexander
  ,, Bell, Joseph
C.S.M. Bell, John
R'man. Bell, William
  ,, Brides, Michael
  ,, Brown, James
Cpl. Bushe, James Hy.
R'man. Campbell, Wm. Saml.
C.M.S. Caton, Jack
R'man. Ceaser, Hugh
  ,, Clarke, Arthur
  ,, Cairns, Robert
  ,, Calvert, William
  ,, Campbell, James
  ,, Campbell, John Hy.
  ,, Caskery, Francis
  ,, Cathcart, Thomas
  ,, Chapman, Jos.
  ,, Chapman, William
  ,, Christie, Jos.
  ,, Clarke, Hugh
  ,, Clarke, William
  ,, Clarke, Wm. Robt.
  ,, Cooper William
  ,, Coulter, James
Sgt. Chambers, Jas. Orr
R'man. Chambers, Robert
  ,, Chapman, David
  ,, Chapman, James
L/Cpl. Chapman, Joseph
R'man. Chapman, William
  ,, Clarke, Chas.
  ,, Clarke, George
Sgt. Clarke, Joseph
R'man. Cleland, George
  ,, Coburn, James
  ,, Coburn, John
  ,, Collington, Edward
  ,, Connolly, John
  ,, Connor, James

R'man. Conway, William Chas.
  ,, Cordiner, Samuel
  ,, Cordner, George
  ,, Cordiner, Thomas
Cpl. Corkin, Hy.
R'man. Corkin, John J.
Cpl. Corken, Robert J.
R'man. Corkin, William
  ,, Corry, John
  ,, Cowan, Albert Wm.
  ,, Cowan, Joseph
  ,, Cowan, Samuel
  ,, Cowan, Thomas
  ,, Creighton, Robert
  ,, Crone, William
  ,, Crowe, Francis
  ,, Coulter, Thomas
  ,, Craig, Alexander
  ,, Craig, David
L/Cpl. Crooks, Chas. Edward
R'man. Crooks, Cecil
  ,, Cullen, William
  ,, Campbell, Edward
  ,, Cassidy, Joseph
Cpl. Cathcart, David
R'man. Chambers, James
Cpl. Cairns, Edward
R'man. Cairns, Samuel
Sgt. Cairns, Thos. John
R'man. Campbell, John
C.Q.M.S. Campbell, William
R'man. Carson, Robert
  ,, Carson, William
  ,, Caughey, Joseph
  ,, Chapman, Arthur
  ,, Clarke, Alfred James
  ,, Clarke, John
  ,, Clay, John
  ,, Colvin, Robert John
  ,, Crawford, William Jas.
Sgt. Cree, John
L/Cpl. Crockard, James
Cpl. Croft, John
R'man. Crone, Richard
  ,, Crothers, James
  ,, Crothers, Robt. James
  ,, Crowe, Fred
  ,, Crowe, John
  ,, Crowe, Thomas
  ,, Crozier, William
Sgt. Crump, William
R'man. Curry, William

R'man. Christie, William John
Sgt. Clarke, William
Sgt. Clendinning, John
R'man. Cochrane, George
,, Colvin, Samuel
,, Corken, Thomas
,, Cowan, Archie
,, Craig, James
,, Cunningham, Dl.
,, Currie, Robert
,, Dalton, David
,, Davidson, James Hall
,, Dodds, Samuel
,, Doherty, Alexander
Sgt. Donnelly, James
R'man. Douglas, Saml. James
,, Dowds, Joseph Hy.
,, Dowling, Albert
,, Drennan, David
L/Cpl. Dunlop, Quinton
R'man. Dunlop, William
,, Davison, Clem.
,, Dawson, John
,, Dempster, George
,, Dobbin, William H.
,, Doole, Isaac
,, Doole, William John
,, Drennan, Robert
,, Dalton, Arthur
,, Dalton, Thomas
,, Dennison, David
,, Dick, Samuel
,, Dickson, Samuel
,, Dole, George
,, Doyle, James Hy.
,, Duffy, Robert John
,, Dunleavy, James
,, Dickson, Chas.
Sgt. Dickson, William G.
R'man. Dodds, John
,, Doherty, Samuel
,, Dowling, Abraham
,, Duff, Joseph
,, Dunbar, Francis
,, Ederton, Henry
,, Elkin, Hugh Kelly
,, English, Alexander
,, English, William Jas.
L/Cpl. Ewart, William Henry
,, Eakin, Thomas
,, Edgar, John
R'man. Elliott, Samuel

R'man. Ellis, Samuel
,, English, Thomas
,, Erwin, Frank
,, Esler, Robert
,, Ewart, Henry
,, Ewart, Henry
,, Ellis, William
,, English, Thomas
,, English, Joseph
Cpl. Fleming, Henry
L/Cpl. Fleming, Robert
R'man. Fleming, Thomas
,, Foster, William
,, Francey, Robt. James
,, French, George
,, French, John
,, Finlay, Hy.
L/Cpl. Fleming, John
,, Fleming, Samuel
R'man. Foster, Allen
,, Foster, John B.
,, Francey, William Jn.
,, Fullerton, Francis
,, Fleming, James
,, Fenton, John
,, Ferrin, Joseph
,, Flannagan, William
,, Fleming, William
,, Fox, William John
,, Foye, Silias
,, Fraser, Robert
,, Freeland, Samuel
L/Cpl. Fulton, John
R'man. Ferguson, Andrew
L/Cpl. Fisher, David
R'man. Fisher, Joseph
,, Foreman, Joseph
,, Forsythe, Fred
,, Forsythe, James
,, Frayer, George
,, Frazer, Robert
,, Gorman James
,, Gausson, Chas. F.
,, Geddis, David
,, Gill, David
,, Gill, William
,, Gillian, William
,, Gillian, William
,, Gordon, Robert
,, Graham, Thomas
Sgt. Graham, William Jn.
R'man. Green, Thomas

R'man, Greene, Joseph
L/Sgt. Gillespie, George
R'man. Gill, Robert
,, Gorman, John
Sgt. Goulding, Fred E.
R'man. Gaston, Alex.
,, Gilmore, Thomas
,, Gowdy, Alex.
,, Graham, James
,, Graham, William
,, Graham, William Jn.
,, Grattan, Hugh
,, Gray, Robt. Jn.
,, Gregory, Joseph
   Griffin, Martin
,, Galbraith, William
,, Galway, Alex.
L/Cpl. Gleghorn, David
R'man. Goudy, Jos.
L/Cpl. Gourlay, David
C.Q.M.S. Gourlay, David H. J.
R'man. Graham, David
,, Graham, William
,, Greene, David
,, Greene, William John
,, Greer, Archibald
L/Cpl. Glendinning, Dd.
R'man. Gordon, James
,, Gorman, Daniel
L/Cpl. Gorman, Phillip
R'man. Goudy, James
,, Goudy, Jos. Hy.
,, Graham, John
,, Graham, Robert
,, Gray, Samuel
Cpl. Gray, William
Sgt. Gregg, Samuel
R'man. Hanna, Boyd
,, Hanna, Fk. James
,, Hanna, Robert
,, Harvey, John
, Haslett, George
, Hawthorn, James
,, Hayes, William James
,, Heasley, William
,, Herron, John
,, Higginson, William Jas.
,, Hill, Thomas Robert
,, Hillis, John
,, Hodgin, John
,, Holmes, George
,, Hull, George Hy.

R'man. Hunter, Robert
,, Hamill, John
Sgt. Harbinson, James
R'man. Harbinson, Rd.
,, Harbinson, William
R.S.M. Hall, Isaac
R'man. Heaney, Thomas
,, Heaney, William E.
,, Hyndman, James
,, Hyndman, Robt. Jn.
,, Haithwaite, C. J. G. M.
,, Hamill, John Edward
Cpl. Hamill, Samuel
R'man. Hamilton, Francis
,, Hamilton, James
,, Hamilton, Thomas J
,, Hanlon, Alex. T.
,, Hanna, Robert
,, Hanna, James
L/Cpl. Hannon, James
R'man. Hannon, Samuel
,, Harvey, Jos. S.
,, Henderson, John
Cpl. Herdman, James
R'man. Hewitt, William John
,, Hogg, James
,, Houston, John
,, Houston, Robert
,, Houston, Robert
,, Hughes, James
L/Cpl. Hume, James
R'man. Ingram, Henry
,, Irvine, David
,, Irvine, John
,, Irvine, James
,, Irvine, John
,, Irvine, Robert
,, Irvine, William
,, Johnston, George
,, Jenkins, Thomas
,, Johnston, David
L/Cpl. Johnston, George
Sgt. Jamison, John
R'man, Jefferson, Walter
,, Johnston, John
,, Johnston, William
,, Jackson, Samuel
,, Johnston, John
,, Johnston, Robert
,, Johnston, William
,, Linton, William
,, Linton, John

R'man. Lyle, Samuel
,, Lyttle, Francis
,, Lyttle, Thomas
,, Lamont, William
,, Lamour, Alex.
Cpl. Lavery, Alex.
R'man. Lavery, James
,, Lavery, John
Sgt. Lavery, William
R'man. Lavery, William John
L/Cpl. Leathem, John
R'man. Leathem, William
,, Leckey, William
,, Lennox, Fk. John
,, Lewis, George
,, Logan, Thomas
,, Lynass, Matt
,, Lynch, Edward Watson
,, Lyness, Chas.
,, Lyness, Thomas
,, Lyttle, Samuel
,, Lightbody, James
,, Lavery, Joseph
,, Lennon, James
,, Lewis, Edward
,, Lewis, William John
,, Lockhart, Robert
,, Logan, Thomas
,, Long, Richardson
,, Lowery, Henry
Sgt. Lavery, George
L/Cpl. Leach, Arnold
R'man. Leathem, William
,, Lennon, Osmond
,, Lewis, James
Cpl. Lindop, Charles
R'man. Lindsay, Hugh
,, Lindsay, Hugh
,, Lindsay, William
,, Logan, John
,, Logan William
,, Lowery, John
,, Luke, Archibald
L/Cpl. Lyle, John
R'man. Lyness, Charles
,, Lyttle, John
L/Cpl. Lunn, James
R'man. Lyness, James
,, Lyons, Thomas
,, Magill, Thomas
,, Mairs, William J.
,, Manning, Reg. Jos.

R'man. Marcus, Alexander
,, Mawhinney, Robt. J.
,, Miller, Hugh
,, Miller, James
,, Miller, John
,, Miller, John
,, Marshall, A.
,, Magill, William
,, Maginnis, John
,, Maginnis, Robert
,, Maginnis, William
,, Marks, Robert
,, Marshall, Andrew
,, Marks, Alexander
,, Marks, Thomas
,, Marwood, James
,, Matchett, James Hy.
,, May, Nathaniel
,, Megarry, Jos. Edward
,, Megrath, William
,, Minford, Alfred
R.Q.M.S. Moore, Richard
R'man. Moore, Robert
,, Moore, William Geo.
,, Morrow, John
,, Mount, James
,, Mulholland, Albert
,, Mulholland, Thos. Jn.
L/Sgt. Munn, Henry
R'man. Murdock, Henry
,, Murdock, Samuel
,, Murphy, Thomas
,, Morrow, James
Cpl. Marsden, James
R'man. Martin, David
,, Martin, Samuel
,, Mather, Joseph
,, Matier, John
L/Cpl. Matier, Thomas
Cpl. Mearns, Jas. Wilson
R'man. Megarry, James
L/Cpl. Mercer, James
R'man. Miller, James
,, Mooney, Robert
,, Moore, Henry
,, Moore, James
,, Moore, William
,, Morrison, William
,, Morrow, James
,, Mynes, Charles
,, Miller, Samuel
L/Sgt. Miller, William

94

R'man. Miller, William
,, Milligan, David
,, Milligan, James H.
,, Milliken, Thomas C. C.
,, Moffat, Samuel
,, Montgomery, Jos.
,, Moore, Herbert J.
,, Moore, John
,, Moore, Walter
L/Sgt. Mulholland, Hugh
R'man. Mulree, Joseph
,, M'Aloney, William
,, M'Bride, Thomas
L/Cpl. M'Burney, John C.
,, M'Burney, Thomas
Cpl. M'Callen, James
R'man. M'Calmont, Wm. J.
,, Martin, Hy.
,, Martin, Thomas
,, Matier, Robert
,, Maxwell, James
,, Megran, Thomas
,, Mills, Samuel
Sgt. Mitchell, Aty. W.
R'man. Moag, David
L/Cpl. Moles, Hy. Smyth
R'man. Mooney, Alex.
,, Moore, Alex.
Sgt. Moore, John
R'man. Moore, Norman Wilfred
,, Moore, William Alex.
,, Morgan, John
,, Morrison, Geo. Thomas
,, Morrow, Robert
,, Morrow, Wm. Hy.
,, Mulholland, Chas. Wm.
,, Mulholland, James
,, Malligan, Jn.
,, Murdock, John
,, Murdock, Thomas
,, M'Allister, Pierce
,, M'Allister, William
,, M'Avoy, Lewis Patton
,, M'Cann, Edward
,, M'Carthy, Jn.
,, M'Caw, James
,, M'Cleery, Samuel
,, M'Cleeland, William
,, M'Cloy, Hy.
,, M'Cartney, John
,, M'Clintock, Thomas
,, M'Clure, William
,, M'Connell, John

R'man. M'Coy, William
,, M'Donald, James
,, M'Dowell, Johnston
,, M'Fadden, John
,, M'Fadden, William
,, M'Crubb, Daniel
,, M'Crugan, Hugh
,, M'Ilwaine, Thomas
,, M'Ivor, Samuel
,, M'Kee, James
,, M'Andrews, H.
,, M'Bride, Alexander
,, M'Cabe, Robert
,, M'Cauley, Robert
,, M'Clelland, John
,, M'Clements, William
,, M'Clenahan, John
,, M'Clenaghan, Rd.
Sgt. M'Clenaghan, Wm. Jas.
R'man. M'Clurg, Adam
,, M'Kee, John
,, M'Kee, Robert
,, M'Kee, William
,, M'Kelvey, Matt
,, M'Lean, William
,, M'Lean, William
,, M'Mullen, Samuel
Cpl. M'Murray, James
R'man. M'Veigh, William
,, M'Aleece, James
,, M'Allister, Charles
,, M'Allister, Jos.
,, M'Auley, Chas.
,, M'Cartney, John
,, M'Clean, John
,, M'Clelland, Samuel
,, M'Cloy, William
L/Cpl. M'Comb, Edward
R'man. M'Corkey, Matt. Geo.
Cpl. M'Cord, Archie
R'man. M'Court, John M.
,, M'Dowell, William
,, M'Dowell, William
,, M'Gimpsey, Jas.
,, M'Grath, Joseph
,, M'Ilroy, Henry
,, M'Intosh, Patrick
L/Cpl. M'Kee, John
R'man. M'Kee, John
,, M'Kee, William
L/Sgt. M'Keown, William
R'man. M'Kibbin, Langtry
,, M'Kibben, Rt. Millar

R'man. M'Kinney, David
,, M'Knight, Alex.
,, M'Knight, William John
,, M'Mullen, James
,, M'Pherson, Robert
L/Sgt. M'Quillan, William
L/Cpl. M'Clurg, William
R'man. M'Comb, Francis
,, M'Comb, James
,, M'Comb, John
,, M'Cormick, Joseph
,, M'Cracken, William
Cpl. M'Cready, Robert
R'man. M'Cullough, Andy
,, M'Cune, James
,, M'Curry, Thomas
,, M'Curley, Felix
,, M'Curley, James
,, M'Donald, Joseph
,, M'Donald, Samuel
,, M'Donald, William
,, M'Dowell, Thomas
,, M'Gurk, John
,, M'Henry, John
,, M'Ilroy, Edward
,, M'Ilroy, Roger
L/Cpl. M'Kechnie, Robert
R'man. M'Keown, Wm. Robt.
,, M'Kibbin, Eli
,, M'Knight, Robert
,, M'Larnan, George
,, M'Murray, William
,, M'Nair, William
,, M'Veigh, William
,, M'Williams, Fredk.
,, M'Williams, John
,, Neill, Thomas
,, M'Cloy, James
,, M'Clure, Thomas Jas.
,, M'Comb, William
,, M'Comiskey, Hbt.
,, M'Donald, Wm. Ed.
,, M'Geown, Samuel
,, M'Ilroy, James
,, M'Kaveney, John
,, M'Keaveney, James
,, M'Keaveney, David
,, M'Keown, William
Cpl. M'Mullen, William
L/Cpl. M'Mullen, Samuel
R'man. M'Nair, John
,, M'Neice, Edward
,, M'Neice, James

R'man. M'Neill, Robert
,, M'Watters, Alex.
,, M'Watters, Alex.
,, Nash, Thomas
,, Neagle, William Jas.
,, Nicholson, John
,, Nolan, Rd. John
,, Neeson, John
,, Neill, John
,, Nelson, Robert
,, Nicholl, Samuel
,, Nicholl, Wm. Hy.
,, Nixon, Robt. Wm.
,, Norwood, Joseph
,, Newell, Thomas
,, Nicholl, Samuel
Cpl. Orr, George
R'man. Orr, Robert Jas.
Cpl. Partridge, John
R'man. Patterson, John
,, Patterson, Thomas
,, Patterson, William
,, Peel, Michael Jos.
Cpl. Phillips, John
R'man. Poots, William
,, Purdy, Samuel
,, O'Neill, James
,, O'Neill, Hugh
,, Orr, John
,, O'Neill, Edward
,, Orr, William John
,, Osborne, William
,, Patterson, Robert
,, Patterson, Thomas
,, Patton, Daniel
,, Peel, Albert
,, Pollock, James
,, Pollock, James
,, Pollock, Samuel
,, Pershaw, John
,, Pritchard, Thomas
,, Purdy, Robert
,, Patterson, James
,, Patterson, Charles
,, Patterson, Samuel
,, Patterson, Thomas
Sgt. Patton, James
R'man. Potts, Stewart
,, Parker, Hugh
,, Patterson, James
,, Pollock, Alexander
,, Pollock, Victor
,, Pershaw, John

R'man. Quinn, Thomas
,, Quigley, David
,, Quigley, Samuel
,, Quigley, Matthew
,, Quinn, Robert
,, Quinn, William
,, Rainey, John
,, Rainey, Robert
,, Rankin, Thomas Hy.
,, Reford, James A. M.
L/Cpl. Reid, Bristow
R'man. Reid, James
Sgt. Renshaw, James Hy.
R'man. Roy, Matthew
,, Raddick, Jonathan
,, Rainey, Henry
,, Rainey, Samuel
,, Rainey, William John
,, Reford, Fras. Johnston
,, Regan, Hugh
,, Reid, Joseph Edward
,, Reid, William
,, Robinson, Henry
,, Rowan, William
,, Roy, Thomas
,, Roy, William James
,, Russell, William
,, Rea, David
,, Ringland, George
,, Roberts, Francis
,, Roberts, William
,, Robinson, Edward
,, Rodgers, James
,, Robinson, William
,, Rowley, James
,, Russell, James
,, Shaw, John
,, Sherritt, Joseph
,, Sinclair, William
,, Skillen, William
,, Sloan, William
,, Smith, Robert
L/Cpl. Smylie, Samuel
R'man. Smyth, James
,, Smyth, Thomas
,, Smyth, William
,, Smyth, William John
,, Steadman, John
Cpl. Steele, Henry
R'man. Stephenson, Joseph
,, Stewart, Brice
,, Stewart, Francis

R'man. Stewart, William
,, Stewart, William
Sgt. Surgenor, James
R'man. Surgenor, John
,, Scott, James
,, Scroggie, John
,, Sergeant, Thomas
,, Salley, Robert
,, Sewell, Francis
,, Shaw, John
,, Shields, Joseph
,, Simpson, Joseph
,, Singleton, Thomas
,, Skelly, James
,, Smith, William
,, Ramsey, John
,, Reid, David
,, Reid, John
L/Cpl. Rennix, Edward G.
R'man. Roberts, Samuel
,, Rodgers, Charles
,, Rush, Edward
,, Scott, Henry
,, Scott, Robert
,, Smyth, Thomas
,, Smyth, William Ed.
,, Stevenson, James
,, Stewart, James
L/Cpl. Stewart, Pack. Mich:
R'man. Stitt, Arthur, Geo.
,, Taggart, Norman
,, Tannahill, Harry
,, Thompson, Hy. Jas.
L/Cpl. Thompson, Joseph
R'man. Smyth, Hugh
,, Smyth, Joseph
,, Smyth, Thomas Hy.
,, Smyth, William
,, Spratt, Samuel
,, Steadman, George
,, Stevenson, John
,, Stewart, Hugh
,, Swann, Samuel
,, Swindle, William
,, Shannon, Alexander
,, Skelton, Arthur
,, Sloan, John
,, Smith, Robert
,, Speedie, Thomas
Sgt. Sprott, Robert
,, Steele, Martin
,, Stewart, William

R'man.	Sterling, David	R'man.	Totten, William
,,	Storey, David	,,	Vogan, William
,,	Storey, Joseph	,,	Walker, Isaac
,,	Straitt, Samuel	,,	Walker, John
Cpl.	Swann, James	,,	Walker, Robert
R'man.	Tate, William Hy.	,,	Wallace, William John
,,	Thompson, Jonathan	,,	Ward, Samuel
,,	Thompson, Robert K.	,,	Ward, Thomas
,,	Thompson, Samuel	,,	Waring, Alfred
,,	Thursby, James	Sgt.	Waring, Samuel
,,	Taggart, Andrew	R'man.	Waring, William
,,	Tate, John	,,	Watson, Alexander
,,	Thompson, John	,,	Whiteside, Samuel
,,	Toman, Henry	,,	Wilson, Samuel
,,	Totten, Joseph	,,	Windsor, Charles
,,	Turner, Samuel	,,	Woods, James
,,	Thompson, Samuel	L/Cpl.	Wright, William
,,	Tolerton, Robert	R'man.	Woods, Samuel
,,	Tollerton, Thomas	,,	Woods, William
,,	Verner, Thomas	,,	Wright, Adam S.
,,	Walker, George F.	,,	Walker, John
,,	Wallace, George	,,	Wallace, Joseph
,,	Wallace, William	L/Cpl.	Wallace, James
,,	Walsh, David	R'man.	Wallace, Joseph
,,	Walsh, William Hy.	,,	Watt, Robert
Sgt.	Waring, Geo. Dickson	,,	White, Robert
R'man.	Waring, James Banks	Sgt.	Whiteside, Albert
,,	Waring, James	R'man.	Wilkinson, William
,,	Waring, William	,,	Williamson, Fredk.
R.S.M.	Watson, John	,,	Wilson, Francis
R'man.	Watson, William	,,	Wilson, James
,,	Webb, Herbert	,,	Wilson, Joseph
,,	Webb, Joseph	,,	Woods, Robert
,,	Weir, Thomas	L/Cpl.	Walker, Henry Alb.
,,	Welch, Alexander	R'man.	Wallace, John
,,	Wilkinson, Hugh	,,	Wallace, William
L/Cpl.	Williamson, Hy.	,,	Waring, John
Sgt.	Williamson, Joe	C.Q.M.S.	Waring, Thomas
R'man.	Wills, James	R'man.	Watson, Joseph
,,	Wills, Samuel	,,	Watt, Samuel
,,	Wilson, Robert	,,	Weir, William
,,	Woods, Clements, Alex.	,,	Williamson, Andy
,,	Woods, James	,,	Williamson, Jos.
C.S.M.	Woods, William Fdk.	,,	Williamson, Samuel
R'man.	Wright, Alexander	,,	Williamson, Wm. John
,,	Wright, Edward	,,	Wilson, David
L/Cpl.	Tate, David	,,	Wilson, James
Cpl.	Tate, James	,,	Wood, Walter
R'man.	Taggart, Thomas	,,	Wylie, William
,,	Thornton, John	,,	Yendall, William
,,	Todd, Francis	,,	Young, Thomas
,,	Todd, John	,,	Young, John
,,	Topping, Hy.	,,	Young, John
,,	Topping, Samuel	,,	Young, William

W. & G. BAIRD Ltd.
BELFAST
Photo Process
Engravers
IN LINE AND
HALF TONE

* 9 7 8 1 8 4 7 3 4 2 4 3 0 *